DIFFERENTIATION AND DISJUNCTION

DIFFERENTIATION AND DISJUNCTION

Interrogating India's Education System

A. R. Vasavi

With a Foreword by
SATISH DESHPANDE

Orient BlackSwan

DIFFERENTIATION AND DISJUNCTION:
INTERROGATING INDIA'S EDUCATION SYSTEM

ORIENT BLACKSWAN PRIVATE LIMITED

Registered Office
3-6-752 Himayatnagar, Hyderabad 500 029, Telangana, India
e-mail: centraloffice@orientblackswan.com

Other Offices
Bengaluru, Chennai, Guwahati, Hyderabad, Kolkata,
Mumbai, New Delhi, Noida, Patna, Visakhapatnam

First published by Orient Blackswan Private Limited 2022

ISBN 978-93-5442-306-2

Typeset in
Calisto MT 10.5/13pt *by*
Shine Graphics, Delhi 110 094

035788

Printed in India at
Thomson Press, New Delhi 110 020

Published by
Orient Blackswan Private Limited
3-6-752 Himayatnagar, Hyderabad 500 029, Telangana, India
e-mail: info@orientblackswan.com

Dedicated to the memory of my parents

H. P. LAKSHMIDEVAMMA (1925-2015)

&

A. D. RAME GOWDA (1920-1978)

CONTENTS

ABBREVIATIONS

ASER	Annual State of Education Report
BA	Bachelor of Arts
BHU	Banaras Hindu University
CABE	Central Advisory Board of Education
CAVA	Chamarajendra Academy of Visual Arts
CBSE	Central Board of Secondary Education
CID	Criminal Investigation Department
CREST	Centre for Research and Education in Social Transformation
CSR	Corporate Social Responsibility
DEEA	Decentralisation of elementary education administration
DIET	District Institute of Education and Training
DISE	District Information System for Education
DPEP	District Primary Education Programme
DQEP	District Quality Education Project
EC	Education Committees
ECCE	Early Childhood Care and Education
EFA	Education for All
GATT	General Agreement on Tariff and Trade
GES	Government Elementary School
GoI	Government of India
HEI	higher education institutes
HM	Head Master/Mistress
IAS	Indian Administrative Service
IB	International Baccalaureate
ICSE	Indian Certificate of Secondary Education
IGCSE	International General Certificate of Secondary Education (Cambridge)

IGNTU	Indira Gandhi National Tribal University
IIM	Indian Institute of Management
IIT	Indian Institute of Technology
ISRO	Indian Space Research Organisation
IT	Information Technology
ITeS	IT-enabled services
ITI	Industrial Training Institutes
JNU	Jawaharlal Nehru University
KPSC	Karnataka Public Services Commission
LAE	Liberal Arts Education
MHRD	Ministry of Human Resource Development
MLA	Member of the Legislative Assembly
MP	Member of Parliament
NAAC	National Assessment and Accreditation Council
NAFRE	National Alliance for Fundamental Right to Education
NCF	National Curriculum Framework
NCRB	National Crime Records Bureau
NEET	National Eligibility cum Entrance Test
NEP	National Education Policy
NGO	Non-governmental Organisation
NIAS	National Institute of Advanced Studies
NKC	National Knowledge Commission
NUEPA	National University of Educational Planning and Administration
OBC	Other Backward Classes
ODL	Open and Distance Learning
PIL	Public Interest Litigation
PRI	Panchayati Raj Institutions
RSA	Rashtriya Shiksha Ayog
RSS	Rashtriya Swayamsevak Sangh
RTE	Right to Education (Act)
RTI	Right to Information
SBC	School Betterment Committees
SC	Scheduled Caste

SDMC	School Development and Monitoring Committee
ST	Scheduled Tribe
STL	Social Transformative Learning
UGC	University Grants Commission
UNESCO	United Nations Educational, Scientific and Cultural Organization
US	United States
VEC	Village Education Committee

FOREWORD

In Search of Hope

Is Indian education facing its most dystopic moment since Independence? If it is, how and where do we find the resources to resuscitate the optimism that we desperately need to face the future? The remarkable achievement of this book is that it summons the courage to begin answering the second question without flinching from the first.

We are in the midst of an unprecedented global pandemic. To make matters worse, the Indian state has become more authoritarian and less accountable than it has ever been. It would be reasonable to assume that this exceptionally bleak context is unjustly magnifying the faults of Indian education. Unfortunately, there is enough evidence to suggest that the effect of this magnification is mild, and that there is already much to be pessimistic about in our education system even without the recent crises.

The quickest way to test this depressing proposition is to come at it from the opposite direction. What is the most heartwarming story you have heard about Indian education in recent times? I can only think of the inspiring performance of government schools in Delhi in recent years, when they produced better results than private schools in the CBSE Class 10 examination. You may have heard of others. But how do those compare with the many disheartening stories that you would have also heard? It may be true that bad news travels faster and farther than good news, but is that all there is to it?

Perhaps the most profoundly disappointing story has been that of higher education. Much was expected from it because it seemed to be the best means of reducing our spiralling inequalities. These expectations seemed to be on the way to fulfilment in the first decade of the new millennium, when our higher education expanded at a rate never seen before in human history. But just a decade later, towards the end of the time window when our exceptionally young population was supposed to yield a substantial 'demographic dividend', we are being forced to face the bitter truth that higher education may have deepened inequalities instead of reducing them. As part of a global phenomenon, the 'massification' of higher education in India has produced institutions of widely varying quality, enabling the established elites to monopolise the better institutions. Moreover, economic stagnation prevented higher education from leading to jobs, thereby blocking mobility—but only after having stoked expectations. Some of the more worrisome developments in recent times—like the lynching of vulnerable persons from particular castes and communities—have probably been aided by the availability of frustrated youth unable to see a future for themselves, and hence willing to vent their frustrations onto others even more helpless than themselves.

However, it is well known that in countries like India, the inequality-reducing potential of higher education is severely limited because the major work of exclusion gets done at the school level. Though things have improved recently, high dropout rates among disadvantaged groups ensure that the cohort eligible to access higher education is already biased in favour of privileged classes and castes. A large proportion of lower caste and poor students are forced to 'choose' the dropout option: the boys because they have to contribute towards the family's earnings by taking up paid work, and the girls because they must become full-time unpaid care workers for the household. That is why the most critical location in Indian education—the location where India's future is being decided on a continuing basis—is the government school.

However, there are many species of government schools. The inspiring story of government schools in the city-state of Delhi (mentioned earlier) is about one such species, the urban school in a prosperous state. Though this story needs closer examination, it does give us a glimpse into the future that is possible if urban schools were to receive the investments and care that they have been crying out for. However, the cruel realities of our country force us to acknowledge that even the government school in a context like Delhi is a privileged location, accessible only to a tiny minority. The real battle for the future of our country is being fought in a different location, namely the rural and small-town government school.

This is precisely the location that Professor Vasavi has engaged with for most of her career, both as an academic researcher and as a committed practitioner. That is why this book is different from, and more than, a normal academic book that might contain useful insights about the subjects it deals with. In its own quiet way, this book is both a manifesto and a testament. It is a testament in that it chronicles, albeit in summary form, a lifelong journey of involvement, discovery, and innovation in the field of publicly funded school education. Professor Vasavi is already recognised internationally as one of the leading ethnographers of education, and this book tells you why. Manifestos are expected to be loud and assertive; instead this soft-spoken text manages to be one by taking the reader on a journey through a diagnosis of the ills of school education and towards a possible remedy. And it does this without ever sounding like a tour guide or making the reader feel like a tourist.

For reasons that are not hard to understand, school education has long attracted utopians and visionaries. But the inspired experiments that they have launched tend to run aground very quickly, wrecked by the harsh realities of an unequal world where the haves do not spare any concern for the have-nots. Thus, school education has also been a graveyard of optimism that has promoted a breed of hard-headed critics quick to find flaws in every new initiative. This book is significant because it preserves the valuable traits of both tribes. It provides an insightful, unsentimental analysis of the core problem, which is 'school differentiation'. It explores the contextual factors that surround and sustain this problem, namely community involvement. And finally, it offers a possible solution in the form of 'social transformative learning'.

There is a familiar vicious circle that blocks positive changes in our world. To have a chance at succeeding, proposals for change need to be based on a ruthless and realistic analysis of what is wrong with the world. But the process of undertaking such an analysis tends to rob the analyst of her optimism, thus impeding the leap of faith that the future demands. Here is a book that makes a sincere attempt to break this vicious circle. Read it with the care that it deserves.

SATISH DESHPANDE
Delhi, June 2022

PUBLISHERS' ACKNOWLEDGEMENTS

The publishers would like to thank the following publications for permission to reproduce some of the essays in this volume.

Chapter II, 'The Culture and Life of Government Elementary Schools', has been revised, and reproduced with the kind permission of *Economic and Political Weekly* (50[33]: 36–50) where it had been published in 2015.

Chapter V, '"Government Brahmin": Caste, The Educated Unemployed, and the Reproduction of Inequalities', has been revised, and reproduced with the kind permission of Palgrave Macmillan, an imprint of Springer Nature, which had published the essay in Helen Ullrich (ed.), *The Impact of Education in South Asia: Perspectives from Sri Lanka to Nepal,* 2019.

Chapter VI, 'Reflexive and Relational, Empathetic and Engaged: A Case for "Social Transformative Learning" in India', was first published in C. Shambu Prasad and John D'Souza (eds), *Rethinking Universities for Development: Intermediaries, Innovation and Inclusion*, Xavier Institute of Management, Bhubaneswar, 2013. It has been revised and reproduced here with the kind permission of Professor C. Shambu Prasad, the organiser of the conference of the Universities and Intermediaries for Inclusive Innovation and Development (UNIID) South Asian network held on 8–9 January, 2013 at Jawaharlal Nehru University (JNU), New Delhi, which culminated in the above-mentioned volume.

Chapter VIII, 'Reimagining Education', has been revised and reproduced with the kind permission of *Seminar* (565, September), where it had been published in 2006.

ACKNOWLEDGEMENTS

For a body of work that began in 1999 and drew on a wide variety of sites across India, this volume and I have accrued debts to several people. Hundreds of parents, teachers, students, and education administrators in the states of Karnataka, Kerala, Tamil Nadu, Rajasthan, Madhya Pradesh, Uttarakhand, Gujarat, and Chhattisgarh shared their experiences and views with me and our team—even when they knew that our research would not afford them any immediate gain and could not resolve the multiple problems they faced. The National Institute of Advanced Studies (Bengaluru) housed and administered many of the research projects between the periods of 2000 and 2011, and I thank the institute and its excellent support staff, Shashi, Sandhya, Stella, Vijayalakshmi, Hamsa, and Srinivas Aithal. Several civil society organisations extended their support and personnel who acted as our field researchers, and I acknowledge their inputs and insights into all the work that is represented here. These organisations include: Samavesh and Eklavya (Bhopal), Bodh (Uttarakhand), Tamil Nadu Science Forum, Kerala Sahitya Shastra Parishad, Digantar (Rajasthan), and Deenabandhu (Chamarajanagar, Karnataka). Several researchers—Siya Singh Chauhan, Lalita, Dhuleshwar Raot, Sucheta Singh, B. Pasha, and S. Dharmendra—were members of various study teams, and I acknowledge with gratitude all the support that they lent to the field research, the analyses, and the field-sharing sessions that were conducted in various sites. Revathi Sampath Kumaran and Sarita Tukaram also lent research support over different periods of time.

Despite the extant crises in India's educational setting and my own alienation from many of them, I consider myself to have been fortunate to have met and interacted with five exceptional scholars-cum-education institution-builders: Professor M. N. Srinivas, Professor Amarlal H. Kalro, Professor T. S. Saraswathi, Professor Peter D'Souza, and Professor Mahesh Rangarajan. Thanks are due to all of them for their encouragement and support, and their personal example of persisting with endeavours in the education field, despite the fact that positive changes have been hard to come by.

Over the years, several friends and academics have been fellow travellers on this journey of research and teaching, and I acknowledge their varied support and friendship. Anjali Noronha, my roommate and friend from our Delhi School of Economics days in the 1980s, first challenged me to think beyond my own social and economic background and is my first critical consciousness teacher. Her work with Eklavya, Madhya Pradesh, stands as a stellar example of the committed work at multiple levels that is required to make education a meaningful endeavour. Professors Patricia Uberoi and Uma Chakravarti were model teacher-scholars during the 1980s, and I am grateful that they continue to be mentors and role models for me and many others. Deepti Mehrotra, Tara Sinha, Janaki Nair, Anwar Jafri, R. N. Syag, Rajaram Bhadu, Carol Upadhya, D. D. Nampoothiri, Mary John, and Archana Mehendale have been at various times and phases fellow travellers in this journey. Ann Gold, Maithreyi Ravikumar, Leya Mathew, and Kala Sunder have read and reviewed various versions of this book, and I thank them for this and for their continued friendship.

Several funding agencies and foundations have helped make research for this book possible, and I acknowledge with gratitude the support provided by the following: Spencer Foundation (Chicago), Sir Ratan Tata Trust (Mumbai), Canadian International Development Agency (New Delhi), UNICEF (New Delhi), and Wipro Applying Thought in School (Bengaluru).

For their enduring friendship and support, I thank Rita Ratnam, Vatsala Parthasarathy, Rameswari Verma, and G. S. Jayadeva. My sister, Dr Shubha Vijay, has been a pillar of strength and a model human being, and I am grateful to her for her presence in my life.

Colleagues and supporters at Punarchith, Chamarajanagar, P. Veerabhadranaika, H. Muthuraju, Sunita Rao, Suma Hanumanthaiah, Siddharth Joshi, Samira Agnihotri, P. Srinivas ('soil Vasu'), Raj, Abhisheka Krishnagopal, Dwijendranath Guru, Sharada Ganesh, Sundramma, Ratheesh Pisharody, and Vinay K. Kumar are exceptional companions in our search for new meanings and endeavours in learning. They seek to address our education system's forms of differentiation and disjunction, and for this and their friendship, I thank them all.

Orient BlackSwan consented to publishing this collection of essays, and I thank Debangana Pal for deploying her editorial pen to not only enhance the readability of the text but also to cross-check many references, and Roopa Sharma for persisting with seeing this manuscript to print. Special thanks to Satish Deshpande for writing the Foreword to this book. His own work on the sociology of India and educational issues has been a source of inspiration.

My parents reposed exceptional faith and investments in our education, despite their own limited formal education. Their dreams and support enabled me to have a life that is vastly different from theirs. For this and for all their love, I dedicate this book to their memory.

A. R. Vasavi
Karnataka, June 2022

I

INTRODUCTION

Educational Differentiation and Disjunction

A child who threatens to commit suicide unless she is admitted to an English-medium school . . . a parent who ties his child to a scooter to ferry her to school . . . a school set ablaze by a fire . . . children dying from food consumed at their school's midday meal . . . graduate students arrested for 'sedition' . . . students committing suicide . . . Vice-Chancellors and Registrars arrested for embezzling funds . . . paid impersonators who write entry exams for professional courses. . . Such news stories add to the flow of chaotic events of our times, and indicate that education as a field; schools, colleges, and universities as sites; and children, students, teachers, and education administrators as subjects and agents have become part of the turbulent trends of the nation. That the Covid-induced lockdown and prolonged disruption of normal life should lead to an 'education emergency', in which large numbers of disadvantaged children have either lost out on learning levels or dropped out of schools, is only one other indicator of the extent to which India's education regime is unequal in structure, reach, and impact. To understand these trends and to comprehend the significance of such complexity, we need to interrogate the multiple and interlinked structures that constitute and mark the nation's education field. Social structures, cultural grammar, political inclinations, and economic logic combine in an unusual cocktail to make education in India a site of periodic and intense contestations.

Ideally, education in a democratic nation must address the multiple inequalities that are embedded in the social fabric of the nation. Disregarding the need for such a perspective, much of India's education system is based on promoting the rhetoric of enabling 'development' and 'modernity' and, more recently, formally upholding the ideals of fundamental rights to basic education. A complex and contradictory regime that has reproduced significant caste and class inequalities, the education system needs to be critically reviewed at several levels. The highly differentiated schooling systems—that range from the poorest and most neglected ashramshalas to competitive international schools—the mass higher education system, and the insulated 'star institutions' combine to differentiate citizens and deny equality of education opportunity. Overall, the education system has been built on overlooking the way long-entrenched structures of 'graded inequality' (Ambedkar 1945) work at micro and macro levels to reproduce forms of inequality. Such inequality includes the continued hold of caste-based disadvantages at a formative stage of people's lives, as also the persistence of caste-based discrimination, corruption, and violation of rights even at the levels of formal institutions such as schools, universities, and recruitment agencies.

These interlinked educational inequalities include unequal structures, access, institutions, and quality of education, which define life chances. As Thorat and Khan's (2016) analyses have highlighted, the increasing privatisation of higher education and decreasing support systems such as scholarships and hostels have meant that persons from the Scheduled Castes (SCs), Scheduled Tribes (STs), and the Muslim community have gained the least from our education system. Controls over entry into professional and high socio-economic mobility tracks such as engineering, medicine, law, etc., mean that only those with access to competitive examination training are enabled entry into these competitive streams. Often constructed as evidence of 'merit-based entry', such schemes (of mass, open entry exams for courses in medicine, engineering, and law) overlook the extent to which there are inbuilt entry-level barriers, and it is primarily those who can afford the costs of training for these exams who gain entry into these courses.

The poor and disadvantaged are assigned low-quality institutions which offer no guarantee of future opportunities, or escape from existing conditions and structures of disadvantage. The economically well-endowed and those with high social and cultural capital are able to access and use the tracks to higher socio-economic opportunities. In continuing to uphold and legitimise such a differentiated education system, the state and its apparatus fail to provide equality of education opportunity, generate an ethos of democratic culture, or facilitate social transformative processes that can address the multiple and interlinked inequalities of Indian society.

Since caste-, class-, and gender-based, and religious and regional inequalities mark Indian society, the inability of the existing education regime to address these inequalities is primarily due to the fact that the structures, institutions, and processes that deploy education are themselves disjunctive. Vast numbers of disadvantaged students experience a range of humiliation and disrespect as part of their journey into formal education.

Despite the recent expansion of higher education (456 state universities, 54 central universities, 126 deemed universities, and 419 private universities [UGC 2022]) and the claims of building on the demographic dividend provided by the world's largest body of tertiary-age youth, the education system in India is largely in a moribund condition. As one critic has highlighted, universities in India now produce 'employees who are de-motivated, students who are disenchanted and the campus promotes mendacity and obfuscation as necessary and important parts of life' (Moosvi 2012). Dysfunctional institutions, poorly managed and centralised educational administration, outdated syllabi, inadequate faculty who are further untrained in new pedagogies, etc., mark the system of mass state higher education. Those who suffer the most are students from rural and middle-and low-ranked caste groups, who are now seeking new forms of recognition by accessing higher education and certification. Yet, the overall system, built on reproducing the structures and cultures of hierarchy, discrimination, and difference, renders large numbers of youth unemployable, and denies them equitable and quality education.[1]

A key issue in the unequal access to quality education and the continued dilution of mass education is linked to the vexatious issue of English as a medium of instruction and communication. The growth of private, low-quality but fee-paying schools which are supposedly 'English medium' and which draw disadvantaged families towards them bears further testimony to the differentiating and disjunctive education system. Attendance at such schools and their subsequent failure to impart adequate and quality education have meant that there is now a large pool of youth who are not competent in either the mother tongue/home languages or in English. If the demand for English has created this at the basic education level, then the populist demand for Indian language-based higher education has created another problem. The expansion of the higher education system without adequately trained faculty and the submission to populist demands for recognising higher education in Indian languages has meant that it is now possible to graduate, even up to the PhD level, without the basic ability to be conversant in English. While this further excludes many from the larger body of knowledge that is available in English, it is the marker of being non-English speaking that leaves many without jobs. As seen in the context of the recent boom in urban service-sector employment, it has been largely those with the ability to speak English who have been able to gain such jobs, further marking the non-English speakers as unemployable.

With the emphasis on enhancing access and bringing a larger proportion of youth into universities and to match international standards, the spread and promotion of higher education has seen quality take a back seat. Witness the establishment of 'open universities', which, in claiming to cater to the needs of disadvantaged students and ensuring their access to higher education, have actually become the new economically successful edu-enterprises that dispense dubious and questionable credentials.[2] Several lakhs of students subscribe to such courses, and correspondence degrees are the single biggest source of degree inflation. Despite collecting such degrees, most students (primarily rural and disadvantaged) do not get to realise jobs or accrue genuine knowledge. Such easy degrees have further created false hopes and tensions, as witnessed in the large numbers of the educated unemployed, who are distanced from rural vocations and life-worlds, and aspire for urban and government jobs through the possession of such degrees. Policies continue to overlook such trends and there is, as the historian Janaki Nair (2016: 20) rues, '...a new idealisation of the University as a space of training, as "skill factories", rather than as laboratories for sustained and critical thought'.

If higher education in general is marked by poor quality and its distance from enabling employment opportunities or inclusive citizenship, then its abilities to cater to the needs of the most disadvantaged are further limited. As assessments of India's reservation or affirmative policy have indicated, there is on the whole a failure to provide an enabling environment for the disadvantaged (Weisskopf 2004), who enter through the positive discrimination or caste-based reservation system. Although policies make broad and inclusive proclamations, actual programmes have not addressed the 'institutional handicaps and handicaps in life-history' (Bögenhold 2001: 833), which continue to mark the lives of students from disadvantaged backgrounds. There are few or no orientation, counselling, and support programmes for such students, who are forced to compete with the much better endowed and advantaged students. Hostilities and rivalries between caste groups lead to the labelling of SC students and others who receive reservations in institutions as 'government Brahmins', '*quota wale*', '*sarkari nawabs*', and as members privileged by the largesse of the government. Intense competition over limited educational seats, deep-rooted prejudice among upper-caste students and faculty, and the institutional failure to facilitate inter-caste integration have led to some of these hostilities. Institutional hostility, especially in the star institutes, not only hinders access to disadvantaged groups, but also rejects any proposal for instituting 'restorative reparation' to disadvantaged scholars. Joshi and Malghan's (2017) excellent analyses of faculty intake in the Indian Institutes of Management (IIMs) indicates that out of a total of 512 faculty in ten IIMs, there were only two from the SCs, thirteen from the Other Backward Castes (OBC), and none at all from the STs. Hostile and resentful privileged faculty consider 'merit' as a natural and individual endowment, and largely overlook the social bases of their own privilege (Sandel 2020). This accounts for their insensitivity towards the life-worlds of disadvantaged groups and persons. What is both visible and invisible across many campuses and institutions is the reproduction of the conventional caste-derived relationships of discrimination and humiliation, even in the context of 'modern educational institutions'.

Popular constructions which regard the access of low-ranked caste groups to education as undeserving and wasteful fail to assess the deep problems in the provisioning of such education, which is largely inadequate, poor in quality, and also fails to enable many to break out of their conditions of disadvantage. Further, recent large-scale mobilisation by economically advantaged caste groups such as the Patels of Gujarat, Meenas of Rajasthan, and the Marathas of Maharashtra for reservation status is an assertion by dominant caste groups for a share in the resources and opportunities that are increasingly becoming scarce and contested.

The dominant education regime is also closely aligned to an economic model that is built on the negation of plural and diverse practices and forms of livelihoods and life-worlds.[3] The model favoured is one which premises both development and economic growth on ideas of fostering the transition of a large mass of people from an agrarian or non-industrial/urban economy to a predominantly urban/industrial economy, or more recently, to the global service economy via opportunities for education. In such a model, little attention is paid to the creation of alternatives in which multiple skills, abilities, and life-worlds can be created or sustained. The feverish expansion of engineering colleges across the country has not enabled many to realise their ambitions of gaining professional jobs, nor has the newly globalising economy sustained the growth of these colleges and institutes. In contrast, despite the fact that there is a dire need in the country to have new types of agricultural training and skilling (to suit the needs of a post-Green Revolution agricultural economy), there is barely an adequate number of agricultural training institutes. It is easier now for a young person to gain entry into an engineering college than an agricultural institute or university. Such disjunctions indicate the failure of both educational policies to carry out accurate and realistic planning, and people's assessment and options of appropriate educational opportunities to invest in.

At the same time, the emphasis on mainstreaming persons into the dominant education and employment model overlooks the multiple disjunctions that it creates. Perhaps the key marker of a disjunctive education regime is linked to the rendering of millions as unemployable rather than merely unemployed. Such conditions mean the marking of youth as failures, and rendering them unfit for either their own communities, especially those that are rural, agrarian, or crafts-based, or for the new economy. More particularly, in a context where the youth form a large pool of the population, this listlessness that results from unemployment, underemployment, and alienation is also the basis for the integration of youth into violent, anti-social activities. Often, we see educated youth, both employed and unemployed, who are active as members of right-wing vigilante groups, and educated persons such as lawyers who periodically stand against the very norms of justice and the rule of law they are obligated to uphold (*NDTV* 2018). These instances bear testimony to the failure of our education system. Among those who do manage to succeed through the processes and markers of examinations, university education does not typically provide the perspectives, skills, and scope needed to become engaged and informed citizens.

Overall, the expansion of the education system in India has been based primarily on matching international data on education access without attention to the content, orientation, impact, and specificities of India's needs. As large numbers of youth enter the portals of higher education, the assertion is for jobs, primarily government jobs, or for urban, industrial, or service jobs. The inability of the economy to absorb such large numbers and the vast discrepancy between the availability of jobs and those aspiring to these jobs has resulted in a crisis of immense proportions. The fact that large numbers of degree holders apply for jobs in the low-end posts of clerks and even manual jobs testifies to the desperation that has set in. While the quality of the institutions, the teaching staff, the curricula, and the content are themselves questionable, the poor regulatory mechanisms have compounded to make the education regime corrupt. Witness the unravelling of the Vyapam cases in which the very institutions that were to act as regulatory structures have facilitated the dilution and corruption of standards of entry into professional education.[4]

Despite trends that indicate new forms of access and engagement, the overall provisioning of inadequate and poor quality education at all levels is visible in the fact that very few Adivasis, Dalits, religious minorities (especially Muslims), and women make it to professional and to high-status jobs. An iron ceiling, constituted first by poor quality education right from elementary to university levels, high elimination rates at various levels, and then the lack of cultural and social capital means that high-status employment opportunities remain few and far between for most disadvantaged groups. This is particularly evident in the limited representation of persons from these disadvantaged communities in key administrative positions and in higher echelons of the private sector. The result of these interlinked inequalities in which disadvantages at the family, caste, community, class, and regional levels remain unaddressed by the education regime are disjunctions that mark students, society, and the nation. These include promoting education on the promise of providing opportunities for a new life, but denying such opportunities to a large number of the 'educated', and failing to assure a common platform on which shared citizenship can be fostered.

The expansion of the education system (both at basic and higher levels) to cater to a large and varied body of students has led to perspectives that translate such new access and education growth into objective and measurable criteria (which are then lauded), and to perspectives that consider it to be a positive indicator to have larger numbers of the masses educated. Such education, which in many ways is of poor and uneven quality, has in turn become the source of much angst and competitiveness, and continues to reinforce deep inequalities, is representative of what are called extractive institutions. Such institutions extract the resources and capabilities of citizens, but fail to provide commensurate assured knowledge or skills. As recent writings (see Acemoglu and Robinson 2013; Piketty 2014) have emphasised, economic growth and overall prosperity can be assured only if they are built on the foundations of inclusive, responsive, and non-extractive institutions which can ensure that the most disadvantaged have rights, opportunities, and material advantages. In such a context, recognising 'merit' requires one to recognise not just individual abilities to perform academically or intellectually, but also the background, social support, and other privileges that enable such capabilities (Sandel 2020). Far from such considerations, what we have in India are simplistic ideas of 'merit', as being either inherently derived or individually achieved. As a result, educational institutions and their culture are built on an edifice of exclusion, difference, competition, and affordability, all of which work against the interests of the most disadvantaged.

The recent policy emphasis on 'skill India' reinforces this bias, inasmuch as being skilled refers to the skills that are required to be factory workers, or those serving the lower end of the urban service economy. If the recent emphasis on skills or vocation education (and its increasing monetisation) has become the foundation for the erosion of integrated liberal education, a new orientation towards providing 'life skills' education in schools and colleges is taking root. While such preparation for life is important, the translation of 'life skills' as preparation for an urban and middle-class life, or a tailoring of youth as per the neoliberal economy with its altered subjectivities of catering to market and capital interests (see Maithreyi 2021), creates more disjunctions in the life-worlds of many. What is especially missing in our education system are learning transactions that can 'encompass an ethics of subjectivity, a politics of emancipation and an aesthetics of freedom' (Biesta and Safstrom 2018: 31).

The failure to address these interlinked problems, or to formulate and implement new structures and orientations is now represented in the recent National Education Policy (NEP) 2020 that the NDA-II government has released.[5] Strategically released and coinciding with the consolidation of the BJP (Bharatiya Janata Party) as a political party with its Hindutva agenda, the NEP 2020 intermeshes (albeit in a subtle way) its prescriptions for an uncritical reintegration of its own constructed ideas of what 'ancient Indian knowledge systems' are, while also seeking to promote the centralisation of education administration through a range of bodies and agencies that will regulate education. More specifically, in failing to address the foundational problem of a highly differentiated education system (right from the elementary to the higher levels), the NEP 2020 reinforces the differentiating, divisive, and disjunctive role of educational institutions in the nation. Perhaps the central deficit of this policy is its failure to reinforce both equality of education opportunity and the possibility of formal education improving 'the stock of ordered knowledge and rational judgment' (Schweder 2017: 696). The NEP 2020 and the haste with which curricula are being remade, and history and social texts being rewritten to present distorted views and ideas about India's history and society, indicate that the education system itself will now become the bearer of narrow nationalist agendas. In these contexts of the larger contested canvas on which education is being deployed, one does not see the harnessing of the potential that education has for acting as a social leveller, enhancing critical thinking abilities, or endowing shared sensibilities, but instead observes multiple ways in which differentiation and disjunction are being reproduced.

The chapters collected in this volume seek to provide a sociological and social anthropological perspective on some of these complexities that bedevil India's educational experiences and trends. Chapter 2, titled 'The Culture and Life of Government Elementary Schools', is an overview, based on fifteen years of field-based research in various parts of India, and focuses on the working of government elementary schools and their problems of institution-building. It notes the seeping in of societal culture into the education bureaucracy's apparatus, the failure to reckon with the subjective conditions of disadvantaged children that results in the 'disappeared child' since the child's interests, well-being, and capabilities are neither recognised nor given attention, the teachers' loss of agency, and the learning loss that has now become a hallmark of government schools. Chapter 3 titled, 'School Differentiation: Pluralism or Separatism?', further elaborates on differentiation in schooling and critically reviews the significance and impact of India's highly differentiated schooling system, which is also the foundational deficit in the nation's education system. It highlights how the challenges to equality of education opportunity, the subsequent reproduction of caste and class privilege and disadvantages, and the erosion of the possibilities of education as a social leveller are played out in the extant and foundational level of elementary education. In Chapter 4, 'Conundrums of "Community": Participation in India's Elementary Education System', I draw on policy documents and studies that relate to the decentralisation of elementary education administration, especially those via the Panchayati Raj Act of 1993, to highlight how the attempt to decentralise education management is fraught with problems of conceptualisation and administration. Chapter 5, '"Government Brahmin": Caste, the Educated Unemployed, and the Reproduction of Inequalities', attempts to understand the process and problems of education and employment-seeking through the personal journey and reflections of a Dalit person. It seeks to provide micro and experiential details to macro processes and trends of marginalisation and discrimination that now mark a large proportion of youths in India. Chapter 6, 'Reflexive and Relational, Empathetic and Engaged: A Case for "Social Transformative Learning" in India', critiques the key limitations of university education and indicates some possibilities in addressing these. Although drawn on one educational endeavour (that of the Centre for Research and Education in Social Transformation [CREST], Kozhikode, Kerala), the chapter points to several ways in which 'social transformative' education can be integrated into the curricula and syllabi of educational programmes. A critical review of the National Education Policy 2020 on the axes of understanding its key recommendations and following some of the implications over the past year forms the crux of Chapter 7, 'National Education Policy 2020: Between Principles and Practice'.

The concluding Chapter 8, 'Epilogue: Reimagining Education', deploys an idealistic imaginary to address the vast array of problems in India's education system.

For a volume that critically interrogates the current trends in India's education system, it would be inadequate to halt with the ideas of differentiation and disjunction. The trends of populist authoritarianism, the spread of religious nationalism, growing consumerism, mass media that is now all-enveloping, and the rise of several 'aspirational classes' are leading to a bubbling cauldron of deep social conflicts. That each of these trends as well as a combination of them pose threats to the cultural pluralism of the nation and to the promises of the Indian Constitution are concerns that every educationist and education institution needs to bear in mind. The many shadows on the education system include the malevolent administrative postures that have resulted in the tragic suicide, which in reality is the 'institutional murder' (Arunima 2017) of Rohith Vemula and many other disadvantaged students across various campuses. The deliberate dismantling of Jawaharlal Nehru University (JNU) and the throttling of student resistance across universities indicate how expressions of new forms of democratic solidarities and dissent against the state (Deshpande 2016) have become intolerable to the current authoritarian regime. That roving mobs and vigilante groups can threaten education institutes and universities to submit to their agendas has become evident in the case of several universities and institutes having to cancel or 'disinvite' speakers.[6] The *hijab* row that has recently emanated from Karnataka indicates the extent to which education institutions have also become sites for contested identities, rights, and citizenship claims (*Frontline* 2022). Hostilities forged on the anvil of social animosity, fanned by those with politically vested interests are now leading to intense community-based tensions and violence. That the *hijab* and the saffron shawl should be brandied as symbols of religious rights and belonging indicate the extent to which assertions of Hindu majoritarianism over religious minorities and their culture have now gained centre-stage within the precincts of education institutions (Amatullah 2022).

Despite these significant limitations, education is increasingly a priced good that even the most disadvantaged seek, despite the many ways in which a sense of 'abjection' (Mathew 2017) is also experienced among citizens as they struggle to gain access to formal education. Parents who make gender-based selection in educational support, hiring proxies to write exams, forcing children to attend boot camps that prepare them for entrance exams, selling land to pay for the costs of higher education, and succumbing to touts and agents for placements in professional education are only some of the acts of desperation that mark the lives of many, and are proof of the multiple failures of our education system.

In the context of these differentiations, disjunctions, and the multiple forms of abjection, desperation, and violence that our current education system entails, it is only apposite that new imaginaries and bold initiatives for education should begin. In addition to retrieving and reinforcing the idea of education as possibility, for forms of social levelling, democracy-building, and equality of opportunity, we will have to conceptualise and articulate education as a means of facilitating '"*cheto-vistar*", the expansion of one's mental horizons, for inducting learners to a new kind of universal consciousness and for creating a genuinely free and equal society' (Devy 2017: 94). The journey towards this will be hard and long, and it will require us to rethink several foundational premises, ideas, approaches, institutions, and processes related to education. And it is in interrogating these received ideas and working towards addressing the foundational deficits of differentiation and disjunction that a first step towards real learning and education can be made.

NOTES

1. For more details on the dysfunctional state universities, see Jeffrey (2010) and Satendar Kumar (2014). Nandini Sundar's essay (2017) also captures several problems at the university level.
2. The spread of open universities or 'correspondence courses' of regular universities has grown, and regulatory mechanisms and processes to check their credentials and quality have been limited. An example is

the recent de-recognition of Karnataka State Open University (Mysore) by the UGC (University Grants Commission) for its lack of standards and non-compliance with review mechanisms (*The Economic Times* 2015). In 2018, seventeen courses were granted recognition again, see (*Star of Mysore* 2018).

3. Ganesh Devy's writings have called attention to this problem. See, especially, his recent work, *The Crisis Within: On Knowledge and Education in India* (2017).
4. The Vyapam scandal or case refers to the exposure of the sale of seats, rigging of exams, and overall dilution and distortion of the process of selecting students for professional courses such as medicine in the state of Madhya Pradesh (*The Hindu* 2021a, 2021b).
5. For some insightful and critical reviews of the National Education Policy 2019, see the essays by Kumkum Roy (2019), Sasheej Hegde (2019), and Niranjanaradhya (2019).
6. Cases of authorities cancelling events and programmes under pressure from right-wing vigilante groups, have been reported from the University of Ahmedabad (*Scroll.in* 2018), University of Delhi (*Hindustan Times* 2017), Banaras Hindu University (*The Hindu* 2019), and from several institutions across the country.

II

THE CULTURE AND LIFE OF GOVERNMENT ELEMENTARY SCHOOLS

The school, going to school, and ideas of mass elementary education have come of age in India. Years of developmental activism, international pressure, and the promulgation of the Right to Education Act (RTE) have championed the spread of elementary schools. Subsequently, schooling has been associated with the objectives of eradicating illiteracy and child labour, creating citizenship, fostering democracy, and facilitating economic growth. From television and radio jingles of '*School chale hum*' (Let us go to school) that present idealised images of going to school in even poor and remote regions, the frequent contestations over curricula and texts, to the current co-option of schools into the ledgers of corporate social responsibility (CSR) and philanthropy, the school has found new presence and visibility in the imagination of the nation. The government elementary school (henceforth GES) stands as an emblematic institution, embodying the ideas of mass schooling and catering to about 200 million school-going children, and accounts for 74 per cent of elementary schools[1] in the nation. For a majority of people, school and schooling is a much-desired experience, and for the marginalised, who have been denied access to education through generations, schooling is a resemblance that they seek. In this historical moment when mass elementary education is breaking the millennia-old caste-based exclusion from literacy (if not from knowledge), and communities are seeking the long denied right to be literate, it is only pertinent that we reckon with the significance of the government school as an institution and understand its culture and life.

Sociological Studies of the GES

Sociological/social anthropological writings and the more recent educational studies have been unable to either provide a theoretical overview of the organisational culture and functioning of the GES or highlight the structural and situational specificity of the Indian elementary education system. Issues like the role of the state in elementary education, the cultural contexts of education dissemination, the culture and functioning of the education department, its impact on students and communities, and the subsequent alteration of students' subjectivities and identities and its impact on the life-worlds of those who have emerged out of the GES have not been studied in detail. One of the reasons for the failure to generate a critical and comprehensive sociology/social anthropology of elementary education in India is largely linked to the fact that many of the writings on elementary education emanate from a critique of the delivery failures of the system itself (Kabeer et al. 2003; Kumar 2006; PROBE Team 1999; Sadgopal 2006; Vasavi 2003), rather than from in-depth understandings of schools as institutions. While some writings trace the historical bases of contemporary government schools (Kumar 2007), sociological studies tend to focus on a cluster of deficits of the elementary education system: inadequate funding, lack of teacher training, poor teaching-learning methods, low academic levels among students, and the overall poor 'quality' of education. Beyond this, a range of problems such as class-, caste-, and gender-based exclusions (Balagopalan and Subrahmanian 2003; Jha and Jhingran 2002; Kingdon 2007; Nambissan 2013; PROBE 1999; Vasavi 2003) have been elaborated. More recent and engaged ethnographic studies, such as that by Veronique Benei, which highlight schools as '... spaces (that) mediate home and nation, playing a constitutive role in the daily lives of children who move back and forth between them' (Benei 2008: 5) are few and far between, and an array of issues pertinent to the structural bases of the GES, its everyday culture and life, and its significance and role in the production of subjectivities are all largely under-studied. Although recent calls for action and observations note that schools are embedded within the larger 'political-economy and sociology of iniquitous educational development' (Velaskar 2013: 126), and that the 'Indian school and classroom [are] under-researched making them a "black-box"' (Nambissan 2013: 83), engaged and in-depth studies of the GES are yet to become central to educational research endeavours. In addition to the fact that educational studies is not yet recognised as a discipline,[2] the paucity of studies of the GES is also linked to the overall poverty of educational studies in India, which, barring a few exceptional studies,[3] is marked by a lack of engaged field research and theoretical rigour. Further, issues of education teaching and research are consigned to specific teacher training institutes and are not the purview of all universities and higher education centres, and do not receive adequate funding support and academic recognition.

Perhaps what studies of India's GES have missed is the failure to recognise what Paulo Freire so aptly pointed out—that educational practice is a 'dimension of social practice as are productive, cultural, and religious practices' (1999: 83). Recognising the GES as an aspect of social practice is to focus on the relationships, meanings and dimensions of power that constitute the institution of the GES and the varied actions (not merely that of teaching or learning) that are interlinked with it. So, in this phase of 'right' to elementary education and the expansion of the system, it is only apposite that studies focus on the 'situatedness of schools' (Bruner 1996) in varied social contexts so that the structuration of schools and their everyday functioning are represented in a processual perspective.[4] To make the interlinkages between the larger political economy of the GES and the socio-cultural particularities of the societies in which they are situated is to deploy what Weis and Fine call a 'critical bifocality', that is, to make '...visible the sinewy linkages or circuits through which structural conditions are enacted in policy and reform institutions as well as the ways in which such conditions come to be woven into community relationships and metabolized by individuals' (2012: 174). In the context of India, education policies are not really reflective of the varied structural conditions of an extremely heterogeneous nation (but are representative of the structures of governance), and policy implementation is often not fully realised. Hence a 'critical bifocality' on the GES needs to be directed towards the very nature of the structuring of the education department itself, which as an apparatus partly structures and conditions the functioning of schools, as well as towards the complex social conditions that combine with the structures of the department and the agency of the Headmistress/master to mark most GES in particular ways.

Hence, it is pertinent to understand the GES through interlinks between the structural arrangements or organisation of the schooling system and the lived discursive practices of schooling. This will enable us to locate and engage with issues such as that of power (Apple and King 1985; Karabel and Halsey 1977), the specific processes by which education is disseminated, the orientation of the curricula (Kumar 1994; Kumar 2007), the varied strategies deployed by teachers as key agents/actors in the system (Bourdieu and Wacquant 1992), and the social significance of the school as an institution. In summary, the structures, conditions, processes, and the agency of key actors intersect to influence how the GES functions and marks the educational life-world of those who enter it.

SIGNIFICANCE OF THE GES

Bracketing the GES as a significant site/institution in a fast-changing nation and its societies and paying attention to both its structuration and its discursive production should enable us to pose the following questions: (a) What is the sociological significance of the GES in the trajectory of the nation and of those who come under its ambit? (b) What is the organisational culture of the school and how does it impact the functioning of the school? (c) How are relationships of power and status played out in the school and how is this reflected in the agency of teachers? (d) What processes mark teaching-learning transactions within the GES and what impact do these transactions have on the learning levels of children?[5] Answers to these questions should provide perspectives on the orientation, functioning, and impact of the GES and lead to a comprehensive overview of the culture, and hence the life, of the average GES.

As a state institution, the school is a layered entity, bearing as its hallmark the imprint of historical agendas. The GES bears many legacies and burdens: from its pre-colonial roots as a space for privileged castes and families to the Christian roots of the very establishment of school as an institution,[6] then to colonial governmentality which rendered GES into state institutions, thereby alienating them from local community knowledge, and later, the post-colonial marking of the GES as a site of nation-building. In addition, as Benei (2008) has noted, schools are sites in which the political is produced through cultural and gendered means in modern nation-states. As key sites, schools are part of the identity formation of young persons and feed into the political, social, cultural, economic, and gendered negotiations of nationhood and citizenship. For those accessing it, especially the economically disadvantaged and marginalised, the GES is seen as an institution that can facilitate generational shifts from the world of poverty and disadvantages.

The post-Jomtien compulsion[7] of the Indian state to expand access to elementary education, and the attendant pressure levied by national and international civil society groups[8] and donor agencies on the Indian state to see elementary education as a panacea for a range of problems have given the GES high visibility and located it within the framework of 'welfare governmentality'.[9] The GES, therefore, now bears the onus of acting as an ameliorative site that must address the multiple disadvantages (malnutrition, child labour, social exclusion, etc.) of a large proportion of the nation's population and act as a medium for realising the new ambitions of a globalising nation-state. Hence, through this recent attempt (since the 1990s) by the state to address the omission of free and compulsory elementary education in the Nehruvian regime,[10] and drawing on ideas of both enhancing capability and human capital development, the state promotion of elementary education or schools has entered a developing phase[11]—expanding across regions, increasing in numbers, and engaging a growing number of children across caste, regional, and religious groups.

Far from being an institution or agency through which equality of educational opportunity or redressal of generational deprivation of education can be offered, the GES is increasingly an institution which acts as a conduit and site for developmentalism. As evident in the large body of literature and in governmental stipulations, schools, and thereby literacy, are key criteria/parameters against which the condition or level of development of a nation-state is assessed. In addition, since literacy and education are key criteria upheld by national and international development agencies, the GES has become the central site through which either achievement or success in these arenas is measured.[12] Missing in such constructions is the more important orientation of ensuring that GES become institutions through which equality of education opportunity and learning as a significant social practice could be realised. In such a context, issues of equality of access, impact, and output (see Reimers 2000) should have been the organising criteria, thereby making the GES a key institution endowing its students with the best of opportunities. Instead, the GES represents one of Dewey's truisms that 'school life organizes itself on a social basis' (1920: 14) and is located within the context of a highly varied and hierarchical society and a system of school differentiation, in which it occupies the second-lowest rung. Standing only one rung above the more impoverished and neglected institution, the ashramshala,[13] which caters to tribal/Adivasi populations, the GES garners little attention from the average middle-class citizen or from the benches of state legislative assemblies and the Parliament.

Once an exclusive institution, entry into which was defined by caste rights, the elementary school is now the key recipient of the Government of India's deployment of agendas for development, democracy, modernity, and, increasingly, globalisation. Promoted on the basis of universalising elementary education, GES are sites where citizenship is sought to be crafted and where the goals of decentralised democracy are expected to be realised. Through its everyday rituals, the assembly, and the occasional 'national festivals' (the celebration of Independence and Republic days), and through the textbooks and curricula, the state seeks to disseminate and instil the elements of nationalism, citizenship, and the imaginaries of a new nation. But even as the GES has become the site of the most intense provisioning of welfare schemes, it exhibits the contradictions and complexities of the socio-economic structures in which it is embedded.

Structures of the GES

Regional polity, and to some extent regional culture and society, rather than regional economy, define and direct how schools function and whom they cater to. This largely explains why there are significant regional and state variations in the functioning of schools and in the delivery and achievement of literacy levels.[14] Recent declarations of rights and the range of programmes to foster inclusiveness and access have led to the spread of GES in societies which are increasingly faced with conditions of disembedding rural economies,[15] and emerging complex semi-urban and urban economies with large proportions of poverty zones or slums.

Enrolment data for several government schools now indicate that it is primarily the children of lower-caste families who fill the rosters of GES. Abandoned by the local economically advantaged and powerful, and hence by the upper caste and those with cultural capital and leverage, the GES cannot be considered a 'common school' catering to the needs of all the children in a specific settlement. At a time when private, including low-fee paying, schools have spread (growing at a rate of nearly 10 per cent per annum and now accounting for about 29 per cent of schools [ASER 2014]), as a result of parents seeking functional schools and/or English-medium education, the GES is increasingly becoming an institution that caters primarily to the poorest and low-ranked caste groups.[16] Compounding such biases are aspects of the very administration of the schools, which further decrease the already low status accorded to the GES.

The education department (at the state level) typically allocates teachers on the basis of their bargaining power and based on its assessment of the teachers' relationships to various caste and class groups in different regions.[17] While schools in cities and towns receive the better networked teachers (persons with political and economic clout, relatives of MPs [Members of Parliament] and MLAs [Members of Legislative Assembly] and elected representatives, persons from large landowning families, those able to pay bribes to gain suitable postings, etc.), schools in villages, hamlets, and remote settlements receive teachers who have little or no clout.[18] There is then further filtering, with villages and settlements that house regional dominant castes typically receiving better qualified and endowed teachers.[19] Members of dominant-caste settlements also do not accept or tolerate ineffective and irresponsible teachers, and in most cases they vocally and actively ensure that only effective teachers are assigned to them. Such biases in allocation and variations in school-community relationships also account for the fact that remote settlements, especially of Adivasi/tribal regions, receive only those teachers who are either fresh recruits lacking clout in the department, or have been sent there on 'punishment posting'. What emerges from such a bias in allocation of teachers is the fact that marginalised and non-literate communities have far less power to challenge these biases in allocation of funds and teachers, or to enforce the education administration to address issues of dysfunctional schools and the problem of errant teachers.

Contradictory Pulses: The GES as a Layered and Porous Institution

In its identity, orientation, and functioning, the average GES is buffeted between the stipulations of the state, the agency of the HM (Headmaster/mistress) and the teachers, and the immediate socio-economic conditions of the settlement in which the school is located. Although in terms of debates and ideas the GES is an embattled or contested site, in the area of administration and policy decisions it remains a benignly neglected institution. Periodic programmes are deployed to tweak its functioning, especially the performance of teachers, but the structure and orientation of the edifice as a whole is rarely reviewed or reworked. With its historical structures dragged into contemporary functioning, the GES as an institution is layered, porous and unstable, and yet loaded with the onerous expectations of enabling the most disadvantaged children to become educated. These tensions between what is expected of the GES and what it delivers make the GES all the more vulnerable as an institution, subject to periodic scrutiny and intervention through programmes that further destabilise it.[20]

The functioning and impact of a school bureaucracy are best described as a 'system bound by obsolete rules and regulations, rigid and uniform in dealing with students and staff, ill-adapted to changing conditions, and stifling to men of initiative and imagination' (Tyack 1977: 399). While much of this may be relevant to the educational bureaucracy in India and to those who administer the GES, the dimension of the bureaucracy being 'rigid and uniform in dealing with students and staff' is not applicable. It is the very inability of the bureaucracy to deal uniformly, fairly and in an expeditious manner that accounts for the contradictory character of the system. A plethora of programmes, processes, and managerial practices are aimed at regulating teachers, enhancing learning levels, and making the GES an effective institution.[21] However, many of these programmes are negotiated, strategised, diluted, distorted, or circumvented by key agents (teachers, education administrators) in the process of implementation, and in many cases, the resulting distortions and dilution compound the very problem that they sought to resolve.[22] While the problems in implementation mark the structural problems of the education department itself, the continued failure to address the multiple problems of the school (inadequately trained teachers, poor accountability mechanisms, low learning levels among children, etc.) becomes the single biggest challenge within the education department, which has increasingly become more an agency of power and opportunity rather than a source of respected regulation.[23] The education department's failure, both in its processes and in providing moral grounding, acts as the legitimising narrative for teachers to ignore its rules and defy it in multiple ways. By its overall failure to hold teachers responsible for the discharge of their duties, to upbraid them for their truancy, etc., the education department itself becomes the source of the erosion of the government schooling system.

Sharma (2009) elaborates on the 'internal dynamics' of the elementary education department, which consists of both the 'declared rules of the game' and the 'unstated dynamic'. While the former relates to the open, and often stated and written rules, regulations, and expectations, the latter refers to the unstated rules which are often in contradiction to the stated rules and procedures. The latter also consists of patronage relations between education administrators and teachers, or between the teachers and the local elite. Although administrative and bureaucratic positions at the state level (centred typically in the capital of a regional state) are formally higher and considered more powerful, it is the bureaucratic members at the lower (district and taluka) levels who are key players and who mark the everyday functioning of the GES. While rules related to the formal hierarchy of the key agents are played out at the bureaucratic level, it is the informal hierarchy and power games that impact the implementation of programmes. Why are the GES in a cluster unsupervised? Why do children remain out of school? Why are textbooks not delivered? Why are classes not conducted regularly? These are conditions that result from the lackadaisical functioning of the district education bureaucrats such as the Block Education Officer.

GES: Not a Total Institution

Constituted and identified primarily as a 'government school' (*sarkari shala*), the GES as an institution has little or no local rootedness, despite the new slogans calling it 'our school' ('*hamari shala*' in Hindi, and '*namma shale*' in Kannada). Within them and in their quotidian culture and life, schools are run neither on rigid rules and regulations reflecting the norms of the bureaucracy, nor on any specific or local cultural format. Hence, the average government school is neither a total institution nor a localised institution catering to the needs and orientations of a vast and varied populace. These characteristics of the GES are subject to, and defined by, the culture of the vast administrative apparatus, the agency of the teachers and the ways in which they strategise the administrative rules, and the social capital of the community in which the schools are located.

From the assembly, in which children stand in rows with the HM and the teacher/s facing them, to the singing of the national anthem, and drill exercises where commands are called out in Hindi (*Ek, do, teen*... even in the deep south!), a regime of initiating order and discipline is sought to be implemented, but never fully realised. Far from being representative of a Foucauldian institution where discipline is instituted, such attempts at discipline are only superficial and have little impact on the overall culture within schools. Instead, emanating from the larger and persisting norms of indifference and the lack of organisation, what marks the overall culture of the GES is the absence of order, even despite instances where severe disciplining (in terms of corporal punishment and frequent reprimands) is deployed. From the lack of attention to children and their individual needs and abilities to the typically unkempt environs of the school, there is, in most cases, an absence of a sense of any rigid subscription to administrative stipulations by the school.

What is practised and manifested as discipline is only a simulacrum of standardised and derived norms of disciplining received via instructions from the department, but implemented with little or no rigour. School administrators and teachers permit and encourage a laxity that permeates the entire functioning of the school. From the compromise on cleanliness to the ways in which the classes and rooms are organised and managed, and the treatment of children, what the GES exhibits is not direct implementation of regimented rules of the state. Instead, the manner and strategies by which teachers negotiate such rules become the norm and account for the wide variations in school standards and functioning.[24] Unkempt GES premises, irregular attendance by teachers, lack of follow-ups of absentee children, the failure of teachers to conduct regular classes are some instances where the inability to implement bureaucratic diktats is evident. Hence, the GES in its functioning and orientation is a reproduction of diluted and distorted stipulations and norms laid out by the department rather than the playing out of 'systematically coded rules' (Strain

1995: 6) that are characteristic of bureaucratic institutions. Every GES then exhibits the different ways and degrees in which its key agents, the principal and the teachers, comply with, negotiate, or resist these varied stipulations and norms.

On the other hand, the fact that some GES function adequately despite the structural constraints that they share with other schools indicates the significance of the agency of the key actors. In her study of a rural GES, Page (2005) notes the role of a single teacher in a school whose interest and commitment drove the school and generated a positive impact among students. Banerji (2000) also noted this in urban government schools in New Delhi, where 'teacher effects', as she calls them, refer to the impact that individual teachers can have on the learning levels of children and on the functioning of classes. Efficient and committed teachers and heads of schools can resist or negotiate structural limitations to focus on enabling children to learn. Similarly, disengaged and indifferent teachers and heads of schools can violate all rules and seek personal gains, thereby creating an environment of dysfunctionality in the system.

School Culture and Rituals

Marking and highlighting the inadequate functioning of the GES is the general culture of the school, which fails to make it a site of comprehensive learning and/or a space for new relationships and experiences. Drawing intensively on the culture in which it is located and more specifically, on the broader Hindu and caste culture, the GES reproduces and manifests a dense non-secular culture. While everyday interactions are marked by hierarchies of age, gender, and caste relations, the culture of special occasions, or 'function days' (as they are called), is fused with the specific cultures of local society. Independence and Republic Days, as also Gandhi Jayanti and Children's Day, are celebrated not so much for their social and political significance but as days of reverence for historical leaders (who are represented as deities), or more recently, as opportunities to imitate song and dance sequences from popular film and television programmes during what is called 'cultural shows'. During Independence and Republic Days there is often an ambience of festivity, and *puja* (worship) is conducted before the portraits of historical figures rather than a dissemination of the ideas that they stood for. As Veronique Benei has elaborated, such rituals in the schools share a homology with the rituals of the temple, while *deshbhakti* (national devotion) is displayed in schools in multiple ways. The result is a combination of both banal nationalism and banal Hinduism. Such religious (mostly Hindu-derived) ritualisation combines with dense nationalism embedded in the school textbooks. As a result, the rituals and embodiment of nationalism and religion make the 'school a unique site for the ritual creation and embodiment of the nation as well as a space that reflects, resonates with, and amplifies ideological processes at play within larger society' (Benei 2008: 64). These ideologies predominantly legitimise the dominance of Hindu society and its practices, emphasise a culture of subservience and obedience, and promote Hindu majoritarianism.

'Thin Democracy': Decentralised Administration and the GES

Although decentralisation in its political manifesto is often presented as the most legitimate form of democracy, the pillars on which it is promoted for elementary education rest on the notions of fostering 'ownership of schools', making teachers accountable to local people, and improving the efficiency of the schooling system.[25]

Drawn on idealised images of composite, integrated rural societies, Gandhian notions of local governance, and on the expectation that all people can engage with democratic processes, the decentralised administration of government schools is seen as the panacea for unaccountable bureaucratic administration. The continuing hold of such ideas is visible in the conceptualisation of the Village Education Committee (VEC) and other similar structures[26] such as the Education Committees (*Shiksha Samitis*), in which all parents who send their children to the GES are members, irrespective of their caste, class, and gender, and are expected to play significant and engaged roles.

However, in the untidy world of a largely hierarchical social structure, an inegalitarian culture, and competitive politics, the processes and realisation of such a democratic structure in the context of elementary education institution-building have not been easy. In reality, successful implementation of the policy of facilitating democratic decentralisation in government schools hinges on the available social and cultural capital, political abilities, the access of different settlements and caste communities to information, and in the facilitation of such processes by the agencies of the state. The mixed track record of the various states (Mukhopadhyay et al. 2009) highlights the tensions and possibilities of grassroots democracy in the context of education institution-building, and also flags the various ways in which such local tensions impact the functioning of government schools. Even in contexts where community-based structures are formed, the problem is compounded by the inability of community members (especially in contexts where a majority are non-literate) to engage with upper-caste teachers, and by the culture of political and social subordination that limits the abilities of marginalised persons and groups, including women, to challenge violations of norms or the dysfunctionality of schools.

The fact that the GES is situated within a configuration of *thin democracy* makes its functioning problematic. While decentralised democratisation or administration seeks to integrate the role and contribution of parents, and make teachers accountable to elected members, the due process of such imagined and expected democracy is thin at best and distorted at worst. Rare is the forum or opportunity for parents to voice their complaints, and rarer still the integration of their inputs or the recognition of parents also as repositories of knowledge. While the potential of decentralised administration is high, and several cases indicate this to be so,[27] the tendency to bypass such processes (holding elections, calling for meetings, including parents and representatives in decision-making, etc.) largely accounts for the fact that decentralisation of GES administration has a mixed record. In most cases and regions, the members of a settlement typically remain passive and non-participant members of such structures and submit to the way in which the Headmistress/master and teachers manage the school. But in other contexts, community members do seek to envelop schools into their own localised realm of politics and economics. Subsequently, members may deploy strategies to access the goods and services available through the school, or seek to make decisions and the distribution of funds and facilities part of their own or their leaders' strategies of power, status maintenance or politics. Cases of communities thwarting and distorting rules related to the use and allocation of funds, the recruitment of personnel, and inter-caste commensality during midday meals are all examples.[28] Missing in the official assigning of Gandhian notions of decentralised administration to communities is the Deweyian (Dewey 1920) ideal of what a school should want for its children. Instead, the GES continues to function with its layered characteristics, as an odd institution that is yet to be rooted in local realities (of knowledge systems and skills, of functioning in tune with local calendars, and of having significance in the local life-worlds of people), and yet to address the disadvantages experienced by the children and enabling them to lead meaningful lives.

GES are also marked by instability. Periodic local festivals and celebrations, calamities, riots, tensions, political events (especially elections), government programmes,[29] transfer of teachers, deputations, and the failure to fill posts leave the classes and schools in conditions that stretch the abilities of those teachers who are present. Various periodic reviews[30] of the GES across the nation have indicated the inadequate functioning of schools in terms of number of working hours, low quality of teaching-learning transactions, and a plethora of problems associated with teaching-learning processes and transactions. And it is the recruitment, constitution, and the working life of teachers that mark the most significant aspect of the functioning and impact of the GES.

Teachers: Systemic Enculturation and Eroded Agency

Although the number of government school teachers has increased over the years,[31] their presence and role in the department, in the functioning of the GES, and their impact on the GES remains contradictory and ambiguous. A combination of anti-agrarianism, growing aspiration for middle-class and urban lifestyles, increasing demands to contribute to the family income, etc., makes the position of the government school teacher a favourite career option for a large number of rural residents. Yet, such aspiration is not attendant with any aptitude for teaching or associated with the moral value of becoming teachers. A large number of teachers indicate that it was a career choice out of either lack of options or based on their idea that it was more accessible than others, and many do not consider it a vocation.[32] Their inadequate education and training compounds[33] the problem of the orientation in which teachers play out their responsibilities and roles. Only a few would have been fortunate enough to have met and interacted with any person who would have influenced them positively. The lack of role models and ideals in an increasingly vitiated social environment has meant that for most GES teachers, being a government employee constitutes their identity.

For many teachers, their social and cultural background with its own logic and rationale become the bases for their perceptions and ideas about children and schooling. They often, and in the most unconscious way, endorse and reproduce many biases and prejudices about children, which then become the bases for their own classroom management and orientation. Such biases include: 'upper-caste children should not sweep or do manual work'; 'upper-caste children are naturally bright'; 'lower-caste children are dull'; 'girls should not be allowed to play rough games'; 'chores such as sweeping and cleaning are best done by girls'; and 'government schools now have only the "chaff of society"', etc.

Given the lack of exposure, ideas, and ideals, induction into the system and its culture of corruption and negligence further erodes the possibility of teachers realising their own potential, or fulfilling with due diligence the responsibility of teaching and nurturing learners. A large proportion of teachers is also from regional dominant castes (Sriprakash 2011), and they often use these networks and leverage their caste position to negotiate the rules of the department. By seeking choice allocation of schools (preferably towns and cities), periodic transfer, or the assistance of caste association and networks for gaining personal favours, many teachers distort the education department's professed and formal rules. Hence, GES teachers are located within multiple social axes which mark their personality and orientation, and their attitude towards their profession. A combination of their personal, social and caste background, the imprint of training, and the exposure to, and their strategic negotiation of, the education department acts to constitute their embodiment as GES teachers.

In the growth of the education bureaucracy over the years, the GES teacher is often the key target of administrative reform, teacher training programmes, and the structures and processes of democratic decentralisation. Each of these programmes deploys against the GES teacher a range of regulation and surveillance mechanisms, which are in turn either subverted or negotiated by the teachers. The vertically arranged hierarchy locates the teacher to the bottom of the education administrative system and the GES teacher is now accountable to the ever-expanding system of education administration, and to officials such as the Cluster Resource Person, the Block Resource Person, the Block Education Officer, and to the faculty of the District Institute of Education and Training (DIET), in addition to the local panchayat and its members and to the school monitoring committee. These hierarchical relationships that reproduce caste and gendered deference and submission norms are played out in Kafkaesque transactions that mark the visits of the education department's officials to the school. Even the heads of schools, who may be local or 'meek dictators' (Kumar 1991) in their everyday functioning and relations within the schools, become minions in the power play that unfolds during such inspectorial and administrative reviews. During such visits, the Headmistress/master offers her/his chair to the visiting official and then stands deferentially in front of the person, who goes through, even if only perfunctorily, the registers and documents related to the school. Transgressions, if any, in the form of poor maintenance of records, the absence of materials, lack of teaching-learning transactions, the absence of teachers or children, etc., are issues that are, in most cases, negotiated rather than addressed through any standard protocol or official regulation.

Teachers exhibit and deploy a range of strategies as they locate themselves within the interstices of the hierarchical education department and its administrative/managerial mechanisms. They are quick to recognise and uphold the importance of administrative over academic matters and make these their career choices if and when they have an opportunity to do so. The result of privileging administrative work over academic work means that the ambition of most teachers is to climb onto the administrative ladder of career success. A widespread culture of seeing teaching positions as secure government jobs means that there is, overall, a failure to generate and sustain a culture of continuous learning. Teachers also understand and internalise the poor monitoring and accountability mechanisms of the education department and its general lack of punitive mechanisms.[34] Observing that errant teachers, as also errant education administrators, often go unpunished, they internalise such negligence by the system as a licence for their own unaccountability. Locating themselves in the interstices of weaknesses and vagaries of the education department, teachers tend to see the department and the system, and its rules and processes as inefficient, pliable, and corrupt. What is practised and displayed as transactions of educational administration are often only forms of overt obedience to circulars and stipulations (during training, orientation, or administration sessions) devoid of engaged implementation of rules and regulations. Many of these systemic failures are captured in government school teacher Bhoju Ram Gujar's (see Gujar and Gold 2005) critical reflections on his experiences in the Rajasthan school system. Based on three decades of experience, he astutely notes the government privileging data over the ability to deal with real conditions, teachers' political links and their ability to retain jobs despite violations, and populist policies that focus only on enrolment figures as key reasons for multiple problems in government schools.

Hierarchy and a culture of obsequious deference are played out in multiple ways: from the ways in which administrators and teachers address one another to the manner of their interactions, and establishing *quid pro quo* relations among themselves. Each encounter encapsulates a hierarchical relationship with its clear lines of who is the superior and who the subordinate. Here, it is not so much the application and imprint of the bureaucracy, but the unquestioned reproduction of a dominant culture (that privileges hierarchy) and the manipulation of the department's norms and regulations that become the rule. Overlooking negligence, a superficial reprimand, a warning that is not followed up, and sometimes even tolerance of an extremely poorly managed school are not exceptional results of such encounters. In a similar vein, the contradictory character of the education bureaucracy is also evident, in that a well-functioning school, a conscientious and dedicated HM or teacher is rarely appreciated, and good work or devoted and conscientious teachers often go unrecognised. Such a culture of functioning means that although they are technically members of the education department, GES teachers are predominantly without voice and presence in decision-making processes (Dyer 1996), and are seen and marked as low-ranked 'civil servants' and employees who, at best, must be trained periodically.

Paying attention to such 'micropolitics of teachers' will enable us to understand why and how teachers '...occupy specific cultural positions, negotiate particular value systems and operate within a matrix of power relations inscribed by the discourse of class, "race", gender and age' (Troyna 2000: 134). In their interactions among themselves and with the students and the body of parents, teachers articulate a social grammar which is itself drawn from the matrix of power relations. Relationships and interaction codes vary between teachers, emphasising hierarchical relations: men vs women, upper caste vs lower caste, older teachers vs younger teachers, locals vs non-locals, better qualified vs less qualified, etc. Identifying the ways in which teachers are treated by the education department, and their own construction and forms of strategies in relating to the department will enable us to move beyond personalising the inadequacy of teachers. Why do they not prepare for classes, why are classes routinised, why do they fail to pay attention to all children, why are they not continuous learners? Situating them in the larger culture diffused and reproduced by the system/department will help understand some of these perplexing and complicated behaviours and actions of teachers.

Located within a culture of thin democracy, lack of agency, and a contradictory bureaucratic apparatus, the average GES teacher becomes a pliable entity whose abilities and roles are defined by this configuration of factors. For those teachers caught in dysfunctional schools, where the HM is indifferent and where the larger culture of non-performance and lack of accountability marks the very culture of the school, the continued disregarding of good work acts as a disincentive. In what teachers critique as 'treating grain and chaff alike',[35] the system sends out a message of its own inability to hold teachers accountable and to uphold norms of performance and delivery. Frustrated teachers voice the reasons for their own academic decline or disinclination to perform. 'Why should we work when the negligent ones are not taken to task?' 'Why are the committed ones and the negligent ones treated alike?' 'What use is there of us working hard when none of our good work is recognised?'

The culture of negligence and of indifference spreads faster than that of engaged work and responsibility. An overall dysfunctional school disseminates its own debilitating and negative culture to its key players, who absorb and integrate those strategies that enable them comfortable passages during their tenure. Even those who would have earlier been committed to fulfilling their responsibilities, and were critical of, and distanced from, the culture of negligence and irresponsibility fall prey to this institutionalised culture of insouciance. The system leaves its imprint on teachers, absorbing them into its own culture, which they then reproduce. This assimilation into the system probably accounts for the fact that in most cases, teachers across the nation, and despite differences in the functioning of their schools, have a near similar stock of responses to queries about the problems of and in the school: 'too many children', 'difficult to handle multi-grade classes', 'children do not attend classes regularly', 'parents are negligent', 'there is too much to teach', 'there is much too much administrative work', 'community members are not interested in the school', 'these children are not interested, television is a distraction', 'we now get only the remainders, the rejects, the best go to the private schools'.[36] While there may be bases to each of these complaints and to the way in which they burden the teacher, these complaints have become part of the way in which teachers have internalised limitations to obstruct their own agency and responsibility.

Teachers also play a mediating role between state and society, transacting the state's messages, negotiating and translating its rules and regulations (Wilson 2001). In the context of a developmental state, where schools are expected or claimed to be a site of developmental activities and programmes, teachers bear the burden of additional responsibilities, but these also become the source of new power and leverage. The institutionalisation of the midday meal[37] is one such example. Initiated to act as an incentive for school-going children and to address the extant forms of malnutrition, the Mid Day Meal Scheme accounts for the increase in students' attendance rates and yet, its deployment has become, in many cases, another source of dilution of duties, an additional burden, and an opportunity for graft among teachers and administrators. The reported cases of food poisoning and the tragic case of the children who died in Bihar[38] are egregious examples of the distortions of bureaucratic welfare. Yet, that such welfare programmes can also address the problem of extant food deprivation is evident in the fact that periodic review and re-organisation of the Mid Day Meal programme has led to its being one of the exceptional forms of positive delivery of mass welfare.[39]

Despite the strong imprint of the system or the education department (and its culture) on teachers, a blanket portrayal of the agency of GES teachers would be inadequate as they do not form a homogenous group, either in terms of their social background or in their personal orientation to their work. There are discernible differences in the very embodiment of teachers—between fresh recruits, the middle-aged, and the older (those who have spent more than fifteen years in the system) ones. On a rough scale, teachers can be divided into three types—engaged practitioners, accommodators or negotiators, and the disengaged[40]—although there is no blanket overlap between these types and their age. Engaged practitioner teachers take the trouble and time to teach, interact with students, know students and their families personally, often develop innovative teaching-learning practices, seek to make education meaningful and enjoyable, and are conscious of their responsibilities. Typically, these engaged practitioners tend to be young, with less than five years of experience, although there are exceptions, and one does find older teachers who are committed and dedicated. On the other hand, at the extreme are the disengaged or indifferent teachers, who rarely take classes, who deliberately violate norms and stipulations of teaching, and who bully or abuse children. Such teachers represent, in large part, the body of teachers who are also frequently absent and who gain a reputation as being 'shirkers' (Bhattacharya 2001).

Between these two types of teachers (who are a minority) are the majority of teachers, who as negotiators have understood and internalised the rules and games of the larger system, and who reproduce in various ways the routinisation, lack of engagement, and absence of accountability of the system. They perform the minimum required of them and are aware of the limitations of the system. Their own performance tends to reflect not so much their abilities as their reading of, and response to, the power play in the school and in the department. Accommodators or negotiators exhibit tremendous flux in their attitude, actions, and work in the GES. An effective Headmistress/master is able to get them to work, and yet these very people can become shirkers under a slack Headmistress/master. These negotiators represent the ways in which the system marks and appropriates teachers, reproducing a pervasive culture of negotiated rules. Negotiators work in the interstices of the system, taking for granted the general absence of accountability, the inability of the system to hold them to account, and the limitations of the system itself, which include, in most cases, the absence of punitive measures when teachers violate not only rules but also the very basis of their employment, that is teaching. The impact of such a culture is visible in the extant forms of diluted programmes, outdated teaching methods, and disengaged teacher-child relations that are evident in the GES across the nation.

In sum, the system constantly and in multiple ways erodes their agency, disables their own growth, stunts their voice, and erases any presence that they can have as key members of the education system. In addition, teacher training itself tends to be 'cosmetic' (Dyer 1996: 38) and is largely unprofessional (Batra 2009), thereby leaving little imprint on the teaching-learning practices that teachers enact in their classes.

Based on recommendations that see inadequate teacher training as key to the problems that most GES face, the GES teacher has become the target of multiple pre- and in-service teacher training programmes. Such training, envisaged as disseminating new teaching-learning methods and professionalising the otherwise poorly educated GES teacher, have, over the years (especially since the 1990s), become the source of new disgruntlement among teachers. Based on a cascade model in which external experts and resource persons train district- and state-level teachers and education department personnel, who then conduct teacher training lessons in the new centres (such as the Cluster Resource Centres and the Block Resource Centres), teacher training has become another source of integrating the teacher into the administrative apparatus of the education department. Instead of facilitating individual growth and skills of teachers, such training sessions have only routinised teacher training. Although the emphases are supposed to be on the new methods of 'child-centred learning' and 'activity-based learning', the inadequate understanding of these approaches and the diluted pedagogical transactions have only compounded the problems. The emphasis on reproducing didactic methods without full comprehension of the ideas and methods behind these approaches has alienated and distanced many teachers. As one of the teachers noted, 'From all this training, I have forgotten how to teach itself',[41] an observation that emphasises the erosion of teachers' agency by such routinised methods of training. Teachers feel the burden of the non-recognition of their own individual abilities and capabilities and then resort to strategies that defy the very purpose of teacher training. In addition to such periodic training, there have, over the years, been trends of curriculum overload, textbook and pedagogic alterations, and new norms of assessing children, all of which have combined to further weaken the agency of teachers and destabilise their own teaching skills. Many of these problems that encode and mark the GES teacher are then transferred to the domain of the classroom and to the teaching-learning transactions within them.

Inside the Classroom: Rote Learning and Learning Loss

Most GES classrooms are multi-grade, with different classes bunched together in a single room and demarcated either by rows, or a seating arrangement in which girls and boys are typically segregated. The inability of teachers to handle two or more classes simultaneously leaves the children in various batches and time periods with little or nothing to do. Restive and uncomfortable children resort to chit-chatting, playing games, and distracting themselves in various ways. Long periods of inactivity are sometimes broken by teaching transactions, in which drill-like methods are employed to dictate notes, read the lesson, or provide instructions to copy from the board, which form the typical teaching transactions. Most classes are then marked by varying audio levels, from high-decibel noise levels broken by periodic silencing by the teacher to hushed silence in which terror-stricken children passively write/copy or listen to the teacher. Rare are the classes in which learning takes place and in which explanation, understanding, and engaged learning are key. Consigning children who have learning problems (for a range of reasons) to the last rows or to corners is not unusual, as also the failure to include all children in all the activities.

Class schedules and teacher allocated classes are more on paper than in practice. Teachers take classes at times and of durations suitable to them. Children lug all the books to and fro between home and school, and the class timetable is rarely followed. Lesson plans are still an idea yet to take root. Classes predominantly consist of reading from the text, some explanation made on the board, and 'practice' (*abhyas*) sessions for a range of subjects. Where transactions take place at all, they are mostly routinised copying of words, sentences, questions, and answers, either from the board or the textbook, or as dictated by the teacher. This occupies most of the children's time and energy. Most classrooms lack any exhibition of children's work and are marked by an environment of anonymity or, in some cases, the dominance of mass-produced posters, which in many ways mimic the textbooks in their content and orientation and pass for teaching-learning materials. New compulsions of displaying teaching-learning materials have meant that classrooms are sometimes festooned with purchased or teacher-made exhibits, which over the months gather dust and grime. Rare is the classroom that displays children's work and rarer the classroom that documents the progressive learning abilities of the children.

In what was the first comprehensive review of the GES in several states, the PROBE (1999) survey team identified and described low levels of teaching activity in schools where there was

> ...quiet inertia of the majority of teachers. In half of the sample schools, there was no teaching activity at the time of the investigators' visit. Inactive teachers were found engaged in a variety of pastimes such as sipping tea, reading comics, or eating peanuts, when they were not just sitting idle. Generally speaking, teaching activity has been reduced to a minimum in terms of both time and effort. And this pattern is not confined to a minority of irresponsible teachers—it has become a way of life in the profession (PROBE 1999: 63).

In addition to the PROBE team's seminal report and the now periodic reports by ASER, there have also been several studies[42] that rue the social attitudes of teachers in relating to students. Key among these is the attitude of most teachers and education administrators, who see the mass of first-generation, low-ranked caste learners as uneducable. Ruing the children's non-literate backgrounds, describing their parents as 'thumb pressers' or as illiterates who cannot sign, and as chaff who cannot inherently be educated, many teachers consider the children as not worth teaching. This attitude towards educability, which is,

> essentially a notion describing learning potential—is the most important means at the disposal of 'Indian' teachers to manage their relationships with children and their parents. In the discourse of educability in India, lower-caste children are habitually described as 'ineducable'. Features of their home background and their caste status are naturalised as attributes that belong—sometimes congenitally—to lower-caste groups. This discourse is used to justify the discriminatory treatment teachers mete out to their learners (Soudien 2007: 130–131).

The attitude that children of low-ranked caste groups are uneducable is only one of the factors that account for low and poor teaching-learning transactions. In addition, many forms of discrimination and biases have entered the school's premises, making the school and classroom a vitiated space. Balagopalan and Subramanian (2003) highlight the ways in which caste relations, and thereby constructions and treatment of children and teacher-parent relations, are constituted in schools in rural Madhya Pradesh and Rajasthan, where corporal punishment and poor learning levels were key reasons for parents to withdraw children from school. A survey of rural schools carried out in West Bengal, for example, found disturbing evidence of primary school teachers showing less regard for the interests of children belonging to Scheduled Castes.

> Teachers tended to perceive themselves as belonging to a different and higher class, often the result of earning much higher incomes than most parents. They rebuked children for not coming properly dressed to school, for being obviously dirty, for being stupid because they belonged to a certain community. Children were ridiculed for their eating habits. In some instances, they were made to sit separately (Shiva Kumar and Rustagi 2010: 18).

Other reports and studies across the nation have also documented multiple forms of discrimination and hostility towards low-ranked caste groups and tribal children, often resulting in their dropping out or withdrawal from the GES (Balagopalan and Subramanian 2003; Nambissan and Sedwal 2002). While overt discrimination and excessive corporal punishment have declined (with publicity and departmental strictures against them), salient discrimination despite the new emphasis on being child-centred, continues.

Since the introduction of periodic in-service teacher training programmes, the focus has been on introducing and inducing teachers to adapt and integrate 'child-centred', 'child-focused' and 'activity-based learning'. Yet, the child, either as an individual or as a citizen who must be served, is rarely recognised. Even in the context of being aware of the social background of the child and her/his individual ability or inability, little effort is made to transact with children on an individual basis. Labelling of children is rampant, with labels such as 'dull child', 'frequently absent child', 'problem child', and even 'MR (for mentally retarded) child' being deployed in front of children. Just as the disadvantaged child is typically neglected, the talented or gifted also receive little attention, and it is not unusual to come across bright children who have dropped out of school because they considered it boring, or were not provided with sufficient attention.

What marks most of the transactions between teachers and children is the socialisation of children into a culture of obedience, of silence and quiet, and of passive hearing, copying and repeating, and doing the bidding of the teacher (including undertaking errands and/or acting as the monitor in the absence of the teacher). These acts and relationships make and force each child to become an obedient child subject, and an 'ideal student'. At the end of these transactions and under the imprint of such relationships, the average GES pupil is typically rendered excessively docile, often incapable of independent thinking, and marked for life to being a subservient subject.

It is no wonder, then, that the GES is now a beleaguered entity, subject to periodic scrutiny and increasingly questioned by even those whom it seeks to serve. As data shows, enrolment at the GES is declining, and the fast-spreading private schools (of a variety and catering to a range of income groups) are gaining enrolment.[43] Seen increasingly as an institution that caters to the poor and to low-ranked caste groups, the GES is no longer an inclusive public institution that can claim to come anywhere close to the much discussed 'common school'. A range of new management techniques and practices that are directed at the GES seek to address its key problems of low learning levels among children, and the problem of poor teacher performance.

New Measures of Performativity

New measures of performativity, drawn from the recent emphasis on making school learning competitive, have brought added attention to the GES. Far from any comprehensive assessment of what schools should be and can be, the emphasis on 'learning levels' indicated by assessing academic competencies in literacy and numeracy have portrayed the GES as failing in its primary goal. While reports such as the ASER and others[44] emphasise learning levels and academic achievement over any holistic approach to education and learning, other critics decry the lack of adequate functioning and the high expenditure incurred by the state as key problems of the GES.[45]

As a range of educational performativity tools are directed at the GES,[46] and the continued problems of poor funding, poor infrastructure, inadequate management, low learning levels, etc., have become part of the public consensus, there is increasing discussion on whether the GES is in its death throes or must finally be put to rest. Such assessments of the GES in the context of the new ambitions of globalising the nation's economy have led to the entry of new players, who seek to go beyond the nationalist, democratic, and developmentalist goals assigned to and associated with elementary education. Claiming to enable a larger body of persons to enter the global economy, new educational players include a range of corporate, philanthropic, and civil society groups who seek to either generate a makeover of the GES or supplant it with new varieties of schools. The result is that the GES is now also a site of the remaking of India into a global workforce and workplace, and ideas of corporate management and governance (e.g., total quality management, etc.), issues of quality and orientation, functioning and performance, delivery and impact are now being directed at it.[47] Given this range of structuration by the larger system, the complex conditions in which the GES are situated, and the role and impact of the key agencies, the question arises as to what the impact of the GES is on the average child who enters its portals.

Reproductive, Transformative or Disjunctive?

Every GES seems to bear the markers of different historical makeovers—from the early periods of being an exclusive entity catering to upper-caste students to becoming an inclusive institution fostering development goals, to being integrated into the public aspirations of a fast globalising economy. In combining these characteristics as an institution, the GES is not so much a site of the capillary powers of the state (*voce* Foucault) that functions to deploy governmentality, but is a combination of both: a disciplinary institution and a pastoral one (Hunter 1996) that alters the subjectivities of the most marginalised and disadvantaged even as it reproduces the priorities of dominant class/caste and therefore of a hierarchical and differentiated society. The GES combines in its effect on pupils the marks of being both transformative (especially for those from non-literate backgrounds) and, at the same time, partly reproductive,[48] given the emphasis on reproducing a dominant culture and its symbols. But, linked largely to the very complexity of its functioning and orientation, the most significant impact of the GES is that it continues to be disjunctive. This is evident in the extent to which the GES as an institution prescribes knowledge of an external world that is different from the range of immediate worlds of the learners, which are primarily rural and agricultural, and in its inability to blend or balance external or global knowledge with relevant or important local knowledge forms. In addition, the GES creates a social distance between the plural life-worlds of an extremely heterogeneous population and the life-world prescribed in textbooks. In its impact, it creates a further disjunction as most of its alumni experience a gap between the aspirations that being literate or identified as 'educated' creates, and the futility that awaits a large number who ultimately are eliminated by the GES or who fail to gain access into a world of formal employment (seen by most as the key objective of elementary education). Hence it is this primary characteristic of the GES as a disjunctive institution that forms the bedrock on which recent anti-schooling sentiments are rising (see Jeffrey et al. 2007) among rural people.

Conclusion

During the optimistic times immediately after political independence, Maulana Azad, a nationalist leader, pronounced the school to be central to the very edifice of nation-building: 'A good school is a national asset of the highest value at any place or at any time. Schools are laboratories which produce the future citizens of a state. The quality of the state depends on the quality of such laboratories.'[49] How far this vision and expectation has drifted is seen in the fact that state concern for government schools has become distanced, as has the linkage between nation-building and the mass of people truncated by the privileging of the market and capital over collective institutions and well-being. Catering to the most disadvantaged and carrying the lofty goals of statist developmental and welfarist interventions, the GES is an instrument of the state but is also a reflection of the weak state, which is unable to command complete submission or deploy its agenda in any effective manner, with its intent negotiated (and often thwarted), and its norms and stipulations diluted through its agents—the teachers and the bureaucracy.

Yet, government elementary schools, although state-owned and operated, are not total institutions. Instead, reflecting their embeddedness in local societies and cultures and drawing on the culture of the education bureaucracy itself, the average GES is an institution marked by contradictory pulses. Despite a plethora of rules, regulations, and norms, the GES as an institution is marked by the agency of those who are its immediate caretakers. Most of the stipulated parameters and rules and regulations are differently negotiated. Inasmuch as the GES is a mass institution that grows and marks its key agents (the teachers) through routinised structures of command and control, it erodes their agency and enhances a culture of sycophancy and subordination. Similarly, its goals of seeking to endow children with education become problematic inasmuch as the very dysfunctionality of the system often thwarts its own goals. It is these contradictory pulses that render most GES ineffective entities. Each school seems contingent on the linkages between the organisational structure and culture of the education department, the social background and agency of the teachers, and the socio-economic status of the locality in which it functions. GES across the nation are broadly similar, with only small degrees of difference between them. And yet they exhibit a specificity that draws on interlinks between the agency of the Headmistress/master and the teachers, their strategising with the rules of the department, and the socio-cultural context of the school.

This portrayal of the culture and life of GES may, inadvertently, be seen as just another critique of the government education system, and as also laying the grounds for further policy directives that foster private schools. As recent studies[50] have elaborated, private schools are also not free from many of the challenges that the GES face, and the quality of education that they deliver is not as problem-free as the advocates of private schooling make it out to be. Further, far from seeking to legitimise or support the demise of the GES, the challenge in unpacking its very problematic constitution and functioning is to understand the systemic roots of the problems, so that the continued deterioration and the possibility of the loss of the dream of having 'common schools' are addressed. For, despite its many failings, the average GES still contains within itself the promise of enabling a new life for many; especially those who have been historically and generationally denied the right to education. The GES is problematic not because it is an institution of the government/state (as is popularly and widely thought), but because it is a mass institution that requires much more imaginaries and energies than what it has been assigned so far. How it can be reclaimed, remade, and revitalised to become a truly public institution catering to the imperatives of being a source of generating equality, democracy, and respect remains a challenge. Although currently the formal transactions, especially that of learning, are problem-ridden, hopes lie in the potential of the GES, which are represented in those exceptional GES that have wrought miracles in the lives of children. And the fact that for the first time in India's history, children of varied castes are breaking age-old barriers of caste-based restrictions and a new school-defined sociality is slowly emerging makes the GES a potential leveller and a propeller.

In assessing the contemporary predicament of the GES, one is compelled to agree with Giroux's observation, 'More than any other institution, public schools serve as a dangerous reminder of both the promise and shortcomings of the social, political, and economic forces that shape society' (1999: 4). For India, this must be the lodestar for elementary education: How, in promoting universal elementary education, can the necessity of a common elementary education be promoted as a valued public good? Even as the language and terms of the market[51] have gained currency, and some corporate interests seek to railroad the very idea of government schools as public institutions, it is still possible to redirect and provide a makeover so that schools emerge as responsive institutions. As a young goat herder, Raju (age ten, of a hamlet in Khategaon, Madhya Pradesh), told me, school for him meant 'being in the shade' (*chhaya mein rehana*). While this alone is adequate to justify upholding the potential and promise of the GES as an institution, it is the larger and broader objective of facilitating equality of not only educational opportunity, but of life's opportunity, that the GES must be associated with. What focused policy directives are required, what initiatives must be forged, what funds must be allocated and, more especially, what imaginaries and commitment are required to transform GES into viaducts of genuine democracy, equality, and plurality? These are the larger questions that must direct future endeavours to resuscitate the GES and not a simple wishing them away, despite the plethora of problems.

In its contemporary moment, the GES stands in a matrix of complex contradictions: it has the potential and promise of being an inclusive institution, but in its content and functioning it deploys forms of exclusion; it lacks autonomy from the larger bureaucratic apparatus that controls it and yet its key agents are largely unaccountable; it combines the goals and functions of welfare governmentality but fails to provide quality education to the most marginalised and disadvantaged; it plays a key pastoral role through its current signature programmes, that of the midday meal, free books, uniforms, cycles, etc., and yet it is also the site of much physical and emotional abuse; it promises children entry into a world of literacy and knowledge but erodes the varied and local knowledge forms and identities of a diverse population; it combines in its final impact both the possibility of social transformation and that of social reproduction, but is largely disjunctive in its impact. In this amalgam of ideologies and practices, the GES remains both an institution faced with multiple challenges and one that holds much promise.

NOTES

Acknowledgements: This chapter draws on field research on government schools in the states of Andhra Pradesh, Karnataka, Madhya Pradesh, Uttarakhand, Tamil Nadu, Kerala, and Rajasthan. Field research was conducted intermittently from 1999 onwards in these states, and since 2002 as part of an action research project in Chamarajanagar district, Karnataka.

1. NUEPA (2014) or District Information System for Education (DISE) data. There are about 15,18,160 elementary schools (Std I to VIII) in the country. Of these, 85.06 per cent are in rural areas while 14.90 per cent are in urban areas (NUEPA 2014).
2. For a sharp and critical review of the failure to recognise education as a discipline, see Hoskin (1993).
3. In the rather thin corpus of educational studies in India, especially on government schools, works by Naik (1975), Krishna Kumar (1991, 1994, 2001), Nita Kumar (2007), and Benei (2009) stand out as exceptional. Reports by groups such as PROBE (1999) and Jha and Jhingran (2002) have contributed to making educational issues topical and highlighting some of the key structural problems in the system. There are several reasons for the poverty of educational studies in

India. These include the overall non-recognition of education as a serious and legitimate issue worthy of study, the subsequent absence of institutional support, and the delinking of higher education and universities from educational issues at all levels. Specialised institutes for education have tended to focus on certification and training of teachers (and on programmes such as B.Ed and M.Ed), and there has been a general neglect of developing theoretical perspectives or a body of literature on education in the country. The paucity of educational studies in Indian languages compounds the problem. While the nation is rich in alternative educational endeavours, an attendant body of literature that can provide a comprehensive and critical overview of the educational system and the various institutions at different levels is yet to emerge.

4. 'Structuration' refers to the formation of structures (political, economic, social) and their reconstitution by new forces, agencies, or ideas. 'Processual perspective' refers to considering social issues, conditions, or events in the context of the 'processes' that constitute or impact them.
5. An additional pertinent question that needs to be factored in, but which most sociological studies have not engaged with, relates to the post-school impact that the GES has on children and their societies. Studies indicate that the distancing of children from the world of agriculture and manual labour and the subsequent inability to be employed in the organised sector has created a sense of disappointment with the formal education system (see Jeffrey et al. 2007). A critical and comprehensive summary of the negative effect of mass schooling is available in the documentary film *Schooling the World* (2010), which has India as one of the countries in focus. The alternative learning group Shikshantar, Udaipur, has also engaged in critiquing mainstream educational systems, especially the government school and the new, mass compulsory elementary education.
6. See Hunter (1996) for details on tracing the Christian roots of schools as institutions.
7. India is a signatory to the Jomtien Pact (1990) that focused on enabling and enforcing nations to provide free and compulsory basic education.
8. Several civil society groups have been active in mobilising and lobbying for making elementary education free and compulsory. The work by NAFRE (National Alliance for Fundamental Right to Education), now disbanded, and a new outfit, Alliance for Fundamental Right

to Education (currently active), and others has tended to link the drive for abolishing child labour with that of promoting elementary education and making it free and compulsory.

9. I draw on Kalyan Sanyal's (2007) notion of 'welfare governmentality' wherein, in the context of the spread of a neoliberal economy and the disjunctions between the dual economies of accumulation by dispossession and the need economy; the state to institute forms of welfare governmentality in order to stem the possible tide of resistance and hostility to the depredations of the accumulation economy. Provisioning midday meals stemmed from the Right to Food movement and the subsequent Supreme Court ruling that stipulated governmental provisioning of food in schools. States have then also resorted to providing other incentives and benefits. Some states have more recently included free textbooks and uniforms, bicycles for high school students, etc., as part of the government's support for schools.
10. See Pulapre Balakrishnan (2010) for details on the failure of the Nehruvian regime to initiate and institute elementary education as a free and compulsory agenda for the masses.
11. Margaret Archer (1982) identifies three phases of educational expansion: emergent, developing, and contemporary. Since the 1990s saw a drastic increase in enrolment and in the overall expansion of the elementary education system, it would be appropriate to locate India's educational expansion since the 1990s to 2010 in the 'developing' phase.
12. For example, most of the key reports and assessments of development use education or access to elementary education as a key indicator. At the levels of the district, state, and the nation, such criteria have been used to evaluate and compare developmental parameters.
13. Ashramshalas are run by the Departments of Social Welfare and Tribal Affairs (under the Ministry of Tribal Affairs) and are often treated as feeding centres rather than as places of learning. Although in some states, such as Kerala, the school is run by the Department of Education, and the residential part is run by the Department of Social Welfare/Tribal Affairs, the average ashramshala in the nation is poorly funded and administered. For details, see the report by Veerabhadranaika et al. (2012).
14. There are several studies that note the regional and state variations in the functioning of schools. For example, see Vaidyanathan and Nair (2001) for inter-state details. Studies by Govinda (2011)

elaborate on some of these, with specific attention to forms of school exclusion.

15. 'Disembedding rural economies' refers to foundational shifts that occur in rural economies through processes and changes relating to the meaning, relationships, and agency of key social, economic and political categories.
16. The study of schools in six states conducted by the National Institute of Advanced Studies (NIAS 2001a, b, c) is one of the studies that indicate the growing absence and withdrawal of upper- and dominant-caste children from government schools, and the predominance of low-ranked caste groups in GES across the country.
17. Although some states have introduced computerised mechanisms for teacher allocation, the actual deployment from the district to specific schools is done at the district level, where the discretionary power of the Block Education Officer and the Deputy Director of Public Instruction determines the allocation of teachers to specific schools.
18. For details of studies that highlight such biases in allocation of schools, see B. K. Anita (2000) and the studies by NIAS (2001 a, b, c).
19. See the reports by NIAS (2001 a, b, c).
20. Periodic reviews have highlighted the dysfunctional nature of GES, which have led to the introduction of varied interventional and corrective programmes, each of which layer the GES. Over the past fifteen years, the introduction of the District Primary Education Programme (in 1994) and later its phasing into the Sarva Shiksha Abhiyan (Education for All, as part of the Universalising Elementary Education agenda) have seen the introduction of a plethora of programmes, ranging from new administrative structures, new teacher training modules and processes, to new curricula and textbooks. Each of these has added to the work and administrative overload of the education department, leading to both a superficial engagement with a plethora of programmes (rather than an engaged, close supervision and monitoring) and a dilution of the objectives for which each programme was established.
21. Several programmes to facilitate and enable the improvement of government schools have been deployed. These include Operation Blackboard (to improve basic infrastructure in schools), the District Primary Education Programme, Mid Day Meal Scheme, and more recently, the *Swachh Shaala* or clean school programme, as school managerial practices across the nation.

22. Examples or cases of how some educational programmes have only compounded the problems that they sought to address can be identified: (a) the case of recruitment of local teachers or *shiksha karmis* by the Madhya Pradesh government, which sought to enhance accessibility but diluted teaching levels and weakened the position of school teachers, and (b) the Nali Kali programme in Karnataka, which was introduced to improve overall learning levels and to enable multi-level, multi-grade teaching, but which led to problems in teachers' preparation and ability to deliver. These are some of the glaring examples.
23. It would not be an exaggeration to say that the education department is, in reality, an employment guarantee department, as it recruits large numbers of personnel who then receive relatively good and stable employment for the duration of their tenure. The fact that entry into it and its functioning are also controlled by political decisions makes it all the more entrenched in power structures.
24. For example, a range of studies indicate the role of teachers; see Banerji (1997), Page (2005).
25. See a range of reports and studies (e.g., Govinda and Diwan 2003; Government of India 1996) that discuss the decentralised administration of elementary education.
26. Legislations pertaining to the establishment of Village Education Committees, School Development and Monitoring Committees, and linkage to Panchayat Raj Institutions, etc.
27. Several studies and reports indicate that in some regions and states, decentralised administration does enable a better functioning of GES. See Govinda and Diwan (2003).
28. Across the nation, there have been instances of how members of school committees misuse funds, seek to distort rules such as the protocols for hoisting the national flag during events such as Republic and Independence Days, or deliberately thwart endeavours such as the idea of inter-caste commensality that the midday meal can promote.
29. Government programmes such as elections and census drives, which draw on teachers as personnel, are often disruptive of GES. In addition, governmental programmes, especially those that are promoted in mission modes and which receive publicity, are often the reason for disruptions. A recent example is the extent to which the new Swachh Bharat Abhiyan or cleanliness drive, in December 2014 led to many GES focusing on these drives on several days, rather than on conducting classes.

30. Periodic reviews of GES in terms of functioning are those by PROBE (1999), ASER, and Educational Initiatives.
31. DISE data (NUEPA 2014) on the increase in the number of GES teachers.
32. Accurate data for the nation as a whole is not available, but an indication of the large numbers who aspire for these positions is evident in the number who take the entry or qualification exam for the jobs. In Karnataka alone, in 2014, a total of 3.86 lakh candidates took the KarTET (Karnataka Teacher Eligibility Test), and of these, only 22,899 or 5.93 per cent passed the test (*The Hindu* 2016).
33. The demand for teacher certification has led to the mushrooming of teacher training institutes across the country, most of which do not have qualified teacher trainers or adequate and updated curricula and syllabi. Data for the exact number of teacher training institutes is not available, but it is estimated that there are more than 250 institutes in each of the major states.
34. There are multiple reasons why the education department fails, in most cases, to implement punitive measures on errant and problematic teachers and administrators. For one, the process of review and decision-making is tedious and prolonged, and officials responsible for taking such decisions are often afraid of the fallout. Pressure brought to bear on such officials by teacher unions, caste groups, and politicians often leads to the dilution of punitive measures. For example, a teacher or administrator found guilty of gross violations (such as high absenteeism, subcontracting jobs, misuse of position, appropriation of funds, abuse of children, dereliction of duties, in-fighting with teachers and HM, etc.) is often transferred from one school or site to another. Transfer is used as the most frequent and punitive measure. This makes the review and accountability mechanisms weak, and the whole system fails to engender a sense of responsibility and accountability among employees.
35. From field notes of a study conducted by the Vidyankura team, NIAS (2007).
36. All citations from teachers are from the six-states study conducted at NIAS (see NIAS 2001a, b,c).
37. Although states such as Tamil Nadu had initiated midday meals in schools in 1962, the nationwide midday school meal programme (National Programme of Nutritional Support to Primary Education) supported by central and state funds was initiated in all government schools in 1995. The programme was initiated after some civil society

groups, especially that of Jean Dreze and the group associated with the Right to Food movement, brought pressure on the government to address the problem of extant malnutrition in the country.

38. The death of twenty-three children by food poisoning from the midday meal served in the GES at Gandhaman village, Chhapra district, Bihar on 13 July 2013 is a stark example of how the meal scheme can also be subject to various acts of misappropriation, misuse, and mismanagement.
39. Reviews of the Mid Day Meal programme assess and indicate it to be responsible for improving attendance at elementary school and for enhancing nutritional levels. See reports by the Right to Food network.
40. This classification and understanding of teachers is drawn from the Vidyankura/District Quality Education Project (DQEP) study of government school teachers in sixteen schools in Chamarajanagar district (NIAS 2007). A sample of 136 teachers was taken—they were closely observed in their classrooms and in the schools, interviewed periodically over a period of four years (2003–2007), and some of them shared their diaries with the project members.
41. Notes from field observations; school-community contact programme of the Vidyankura/DQEP (NIAS 2007).
42. Studies on caste and ethnicity-based discrimination in classrooms and schools include those by Kumar (1985), Nambissan and Sedwal (2002), Ramachandran and Naorem (2013), and NIAS (2001a, b, c).
43. Enrolment in private schools is increasing every year. While in the 1980s private schools accounted for less than 10 per cent of all children, by 2014 approximately 30.8 per cent of children were in private schools (ASER 2014), with some states such as Kerala indicating that more than 50 per cent of schools were in the private sector.
44. Other reports and studies that provide an assessment of learning levels in GES include those by the NCERT, ASER, and Educational Initiatives.
45. Criticisms of the GES as a government and public institution which reproduces forms of inequality are represented in the works by Majumdar and Mooij (2011), and Ravi Kumar (2006).
46. A range of educational performativity tools have been developed by ASER, Educational Initiative, and the NCERT. In Karnataka, the Karnataka State Quality Assessment Organisation has developed some assessment tools.

47. Several corporate groups, especially those from the Information Technology industry, deploy their charitable and corporate social responsibility funds in the arena of elementary education. Apart from 'school adoption' programmes, there are now several public-private partnerships and agreements between these corporate groups and the state education departments for improving elementary education.
48. The very entry of children of all castes and the officially enunciated inclusiveness of elementary education and the GES's inability to fit into the emerging global economy does not permit it to become a simple reproductive model (see criticisms of the reproductive model by Anyon 2006).
49. From Maulana Azad's speech at Scindia School, Gwalior, on 26 February 1949. Sourced from the exhibit on national leaders, Nehru Memorial Museum and Library, New Delhi, December 2014.
50. For details of some critical reviews of private schools, including expensive and popular ones, and their inability to also deliver adequate and relevant education, see the studies by Education Initiative and WATIS (n.d). Nambissan (2014) provides details of some of the new low-fee paying private schools (which are also primarily 'teach shops', seeking only to 'teach' the texts in the syllabus, while catering to aspirations for English education) and their inabilities to deliver 'good' or quality education.
51. For a comprehensive review of trends in the increasing marketisation of education, see the volume by Weis et al. (2006).

III

SCHOOL DIFFERENTIATION

Pluralism or Separatism?

Over the past two decades, two important and interesting public interest litigations (PIL) pertaining to schools have been filed. One such PIL by Ravindra Talpe and Uday Warunjikar from a civil society organisation in Maharashtra petitioned the High Court for more information on the deaths of 793 children over the period of 2007 to 2017 in the 1,100 ashramshalas in the state.[1] They cited that no details, including names of the children and the causes of deaths, were available and called attention to the poor state of the ashramshalas, which were supposed to cater to the Adivasi/tribal population.

The second PIL concerns the objection to the Right of Children to Free and Compulsory Education Act of 2009 (or Right to Education [RTE]) and was filed by the Society for Unaided Private Schools of Rajasthan in 2012.[2] The petitioners indicated that the 2009 Act violated Article 19(1) of the Constitution, which gave them the freedom of occupation. They cited that the RTE's section 12(1) C, which stipulates that 25 per cent of seats in private schools be reserved for children from the economically weaker and disadvantaged sections, and rules relating to infrastructure were against the interests of organisations that run and maintain private schools.

These two PIL petitions represent the extent to which schooling and the rights to elementary education remain contested, and there are sharp variations in the ways in which citizens are responding to their own needs and demands for education. While one PIL seeks to assert the rights of disadvantaged children to quality and safety in schools, the other seeks to retain the class-based exclusivity of schools. Located within these contestations, the increasing proliferation and differentiation of schools also reflect the growing socio-economic differences among India's social classes and their varied positions vis-à-vis the state and the market. Although only four types of schools (government, aided, unaided/ private, and local administration) are identified by the government (see NUEPA 2011), a spectrum of schools— with the government ashramshalas (residential schools for tribals/Adivasis) at one end and international schools at the other—reflects the variations in socio-economic status and the affordability and aspirations of parents. Depending on the costs, medium of instruction, type of board exams undertaken, and management structure, there are currently nine types of schools in the country. Each of the school systems/types caters to specific socio-economic groups, and in most cases (barring those in which children attend both 'madrassas' and other regular schools), is exclusive of each other. While recent data for India indicate the growth of the school education system (catering to about 250–300 million children),which has become one of the world's largest (NUEPA 2011),[3] inadequate attention has been paid to the proliferation and significance of diverse types of schools and the increasing complexity of the schooling system. Hence, trends such as these require us to review not only the data on the growth of literacy levels and the expansion of the educational system, which is often invoked to indicate and celebrate educational achievements in the nation, but to also raise a number of questions. Key among these relate to the issue of equality of educational opportunity and equality of educational outcomes. What implications does such a range of schools have for a society and nation in which the social fabric is marked by hierarchy, difference, discrimination, and inequities, and how does it impact society and nation? Will such a differentiated schooling system enhance the life opportunities of all and sustain the plurality of cultures? Or, if schools are expected to be conduits for promoting democracy and a common weal among people, then how will such a mandate be realised? If the variety of schools is reflective of the different socio-economic and cultural aspirations of the people, will this also constitute another source of separatism among the students who attend different schools and educational institutions? Are the variations in schools indicative of the cultural choices of people that sustain their pluralism, or are they reflective of the role of the market, the state, and civil society organisations in promoting a variety of schools? Overall, what implications do these trends have for the ideal of schools being the site from which inherited and generational inequities ought to be challenged?

In unpacking the trends of proliferation of different types of schools, we need to recognise the extent to which schools are not merely sites of socialisation, but are increasingly key institutions that play a central role in structuring and assigning opportunities. A key source of identity formation, power, and multiple forms of capital[4] (economic, social, and cultural), schools also act as both conduits and markers that influence the future life chances of children. Ideally in a democracy—both as enunciated and as practised—schools must be key sites or public institutions that provide the equalising resemblances required to challenge the inequities reproduced by various inherited social structures, institutions, and agencies of society. For a nation constituted by diverse societies and cultures and in which multiple forms of exclusion continue to operate, schools have the potential to become the most significant institutions to instil and disseminate notions of shared ideals and collective goals so as to facilitate the growth of both a democratic society and a democratic nation. But trends in India's schooling system and its increasing differentiation defy such possibilities.

Typology of Schools

1. Government Schools: With more than 11 lakh (1.1 million) schools across the nation[5] and accounting for the single largest proportion of schools, catering to 71 per cent of children (ASER 2014), the government school is a beleaguered entity. Administered by various regional/state governments, there are wide differences in government schools and their functioning and quality of education. Despite increments

in recent budgetary allocations to elementary education and much governmental, intergovernmental, and civil society efforts to sustain them, there has been a decline in the overall functioning of most government schools, which typically tend to be located in rural areas and in poor urban areas. A large volume of studies and reviews indicate that most government schools have poor infrastructure and low learning levels, function for an inadequate number of days, and overall, do not cater to the interests of children.[6]

2. Aided Schools: These are schools that are run by private enterprises/agencies or associations, but which receive government grants/aid (primarily for teachers' salaries) and are affiliated to various state board examinations. According to recent data (Government of India 2018), there are 83,787 aided schools. Such schools cater to a range of income groups and are situated primarily in towns and cities. These include many of the older 'convent' schools and those run by institutions classified as religious minorities, and which receive government funds.
3. Unaided Private Schools: These are schools that receive no monetary support or benefits from the government, and are based on fee collections and donations. As per 2018 Government of India data, there are now 33,05,777 private schools, but in reality, there are many more that have sprouted over the years (see Bose et al. 2021). Depending on the class and medium of instruction (English or regional languages), these schools are affiliated to either central boards such as the ICSE (Indian Certificate of Secondary Education) or CBSE (Central Board of Secondary Education), or to state boards. While early private schools were primarily catering to the economically better-off sections and were based in towns and cities, there is now a wider range of private schools that draw on the outflow of children from government schools. The range is wide and includes schools professing to be 'public schools'[7] (in the manner of the United Kingdom schools[8]), which cater to the new upwardly mobile classes, and also those that are called 'low-fee paying' schools, which are

primarily those that have inadequate infrastructure and cater to poorer sections in areas of urban poverty and in some rural areas (Kamat et al. 2016; Nambissan 2014). Recent offshoots of private educational groups or networks claiming to cater to mass educational requirements, especially for disadvantaged children, include networks such as the 'Ekal Vidyalaya' schools run by a philanthropic group,[9] and 'Vidya Bharati', an educational wing of the RSS (Rashtriya Swayamsevak Sangh), which runs schools for tribal and rural children and provide education to several thousands of children. Most of these schools are characterised by a lack of accountability to government regulatory structures and processes, and many intend to integrate peripheral and disadvantaged groups into the Hindutva agenda.

4. 'Kendriya Vidyalaya' (KV) Schools: These are schools (a total of 1,093 across the country[10]) established by the central government and cater to the children of central government employees, especially those in transferable jobs. Most of these are also attached to public sector companies[11] and include the KVs in metropolitan areas as well as those located in public-sector townships. Since children of all employees are entitled to entry, the student composition in most Kendriya Vidyalayas is economically, socially, and regionally diverse. Teachers and administrators are recruited through open and competitive schemes and are trained and well-supervised. All Kendriya Vidyalayas are affiliated to the CBSE, and many are reputed for high levels of academic performance, and are often seen as models for common schools[12] that can be promoted across the country.
5. 'Navodaya' Schools: Established to act as 'magnet' or 'elite'[13] schools for rural areas, these are also managed by the central government. Admission is based on an entrance examination after Standard V. The 595 Navodaya schools are prevalent in all districts of the nation and have a pool of nationally recruited teachers. Children are primarily from the district; 75 per cent of seats are reserved for rural students, and 25 per cent are for those from urban areas.

While 3 per cent of the seats are also reserved for physically challenged children, another 33 per cent is reserved for girls. There is also a district-based proportional reservation of seats for children from the Scheduled Caste and tribal (SC/ST) communities. A small number of senior students are from other regions and act as exchange students.

6. 'Ashramshalas': These are residential schools established to cater to Adivasis or tribals, especially those in remote and inaccessible geographical areas. Although funds are from the central government, ashramshalas are administered by state governments (mostly by the departments of social welfare), and are marked by overall poor standards in infrastructure, inadequately trained faculty, and typically have low learning levels. Located in remote rural areas of the nation, most ashramshalas function more as feeding centres than as learning centres.[14] Dropout rates are high and many of the ashramshalas are only up to Standard V. Since 2004, in addition to these schools, there are 1,226 residential schools for adolescent girls, called 'Kasturba Gandhi Balika Vidyalayas',[15] which cater to girls in areas where upper primary and high schools are not easily accessible.
7. Religious Schools: These include 'maktabs' or mosque-based learning centres, 'madrassas'[16] and 'pathshalas' that are run primarily for the religious instruction of children. Some of them have components of modern education and some are run as part-time learning centres. While many are affiliated to the regular boards and are even aided by state governments, there are some which do not have formal affiliation to school boards and do not conduct certification exams. Many of these schools draw primarily on poor and disadvantaged students. More recently, we have seen the establishment of some 'gurukuls' based on the supposedly Vedic form of teaching-learning,[17] which cater to the aspirations and orientations of those seeking a return to a constructed glorious Hindu past.
8. Alternative Schools: Established by different civil society organisations and/or individuals, these schools cater to either

disadvantaged children or to elite children. Most are run on the lines of progressive education and are at the forefront of developing innovative teaching-learning methods. Many are not formally affiliated to examination or supervisory boards, and some enable their students to take the 'open school' board exams.

9. International Schools: Although the first international school was established in 1976, there has been a spurt in their growth since the late 1990s. Catering to the elite, the new rich, and the expatriates in metropolitan areas, these schools reflect the growth of the global urban economy. Although some do have a small proportion of expatriate children and those whose parents are on international employment circuits, many of the students are from local business and professional families. Affiliations are to central board examinations and/or to international boards such as the International General Certificate of Secondary Education (IGCSE [Cambridge]) and the International Baccalaureate (IB).

TRENDS IN SCHOOL DIFFERENTIATION

Few images can better encapsulate the growing differentiation and segmentation of schooling in India than the picture of school buses plying children to and from a variety of schools. While buses with the names of schools indicate the wide range of schools available, those that ply in the rural areas indicate how the relatively better-off here are also opting out of village government schools. Hence, busing children to schools in India has gained a new meaning that is very different from the American idea of busing children. If busing in the US was initiated to challenge residence- and race-based segregation of children and to make way for integrating children of different races into schools, busing in India is the practice of shuttling children to schools that their parents can afford, and to move them away from their neighbourhoods and local schools.

The mushrooming and growth of these diverse types of schools, which clearly reinforce the class-based, regional, religious, and social divides in India, reflect the extent to which there is an absence of educational policy that can engage with and/or provide direction to, and suit the broader goals of education. As evident in the most recent National Education Policy (NEP) 2020, there is no mention at all of promoting or establishing a common school system for the nation. Instead, in most cases, conditions and trends in schools indicate that far from creating a level playing field, the growth of schools highlights the ways in which policies 'favour the most favoured and disfavour the most disfavoured' (Bourdieu 2010: 36). Nothing substantiates this better than the fact that the poor and disadvantaged receive the lowest quality and type of school, while the well-endowed receive substantial support. For example, there is no single authority, board, or registered society at the Centre accountable to the Ministry that oversees the education of Adivasi/tribal children or the functioning of the ashramshalas. This is unlike the specialised institutional support for schools such as the Kendriya Vidyalayas, the Navodayas, and even the elite special boarding schools that the Department of Defence provides for the children of its officers.[18]

Government schools reflect their history of having been established by the colonial or independent state governments which once catered to local elites, but have now, since the 1990s, expanded due to the forced obligation of the state to meet the pressures of civil society and international aid organisations to enhance access to elementary education. Where literacy and basic education are seen as key to development and capability enhancement, mass schooling is seen as an unavoidable compulsion. That the schools do not manage to cater to the real needs and orientation of a varied population is explicit in the extent to which schooling and issues of management and quality of education have become contentious issues (see Chapter 2, this volume). Factors such as the problems of funding, management, recruitment, training and accountability of teachers, and the content and orientation of school textbooks have become matters for public debates.[19]

The growth of many of the new private schools reflects the demand for education by parents from a wide spectrum of classes—from the working poor to the new middle classes in both urban and rural areas. Many of the private schools, including the low-fee paying ones, reflect parents' aspiration for mobility and their resistance against the poor quality of schools provided by the government. In addition, such private schools represent the ability of the market to fill the gap in the state's educational provisioning capacities. The search for English-medium education alone is one of the key factors for the decline of government schools, and is both the source and result of deeper social fracturing. As Faust and Nagar (2001) elaborate, the demand for English-medium education fractures not only the fabric of earlier socialities and identities (such as those derived from Indian language and regional cultural identities), but also creates a double alienation between students and their home life and culture, and among students.[20]

Religious schools such as pathshalas and madrassas, including the new 'Gurukul International Schools' (some of which claim to 'fuse ancient wisdom and modern technology') and the new-age 'heritage' schools, reflect and represent not merely the hold of traditional learning among certain circles, but also the reinforcement and re-embedding of education within the fold of religious institutions, and the integration of entrepreneurship and profit-making by and into religious institutions. Far from decreasing or declining, the growth of some of these religious schools indicates a reinforced legitimacy that they have gained at a time of increasing globalisation.

Market and Schools

Among the upper classes and elite with high disposable incomes, education, in the language of the market, is an investment for which parents seek the best returns, and this is now determining their choice of schools.[21] Competition, facilities, monitoring, etc., have become the terms by which such new privatised and exclusive schools are being promoted. Educationist Krishna Kumar has decried such trends which legitimise exclusion, and has observed that such 'super schools are acquiring the character of export zones of industrial production where any normative supervision by law is perceived as bureaucratic intrusion which is harmful for the pursuit of quality and maintenance of the competitive edge' (Kumar 2003: 5166). The growth of these schools is the education market's response to parental ambitions that seek to place their children onto international careers. As a result of such choices, and feeding into the international economy that seeks to make educational credentials a part of trade agreements, schools are now producing 'world kids with GATT-transportable generic skills, knowledge and competences' (Luke 2006: 134). High-end international schools, also referred to as 'five-star' schools, reflect the ambitions and economic capacities of upper-class and elite parents who are able to purchase exclusive education for their children. Such schools, which advertise themselves on the basis of providing world-class infrastructure, reflect the expanding market, and the increasing globalised standards in living and lifestyles of a small proportion of the population. What such international schools make possible for globalised elites, or for those with aspirations of dominance in global markets and societies, are strategies where their ambitions to circulate capital, knowledge, and resources are made possible via new boundary maintenance mechanisms (Bolay and Rey 2021) among elites, and/or between elites and non-elites.

Inasmuch as schools are being promoted with the language of the market, their variations and range are increasingly reflecting 'the stratified purchasing power of different consumer groups' (Jonathan 1989: 322). Distanced from the state and its regulatory mechanisms, such schools are increasingly associated with, and driven by, competitive parameters among themselves. These include not only a constant upgradation of facilities, but also the introduction of new teaching-learning packages which are products of an increasingly commercialised education industry.[22] Private companies and consultants seek to provide a range of 'edu-services' (from development of curricula, textbooks, teaching-learning materials, school management, teacher training, and student assessment), and as 'edu-entrepreneurs' they vie with each other to capture educational institutions as their clients. Such organisations and agents have become a formidable force in formulating educational standards and expectations, and are also responsible for the increasing costs that private schools bear.

The challenges of educational exclusiveness in a nation that is economically and socially diverse are several. More particularly, it raises the question of whether, in a hierarchical, segregated, and plural society, schools should be based on the idea of equal provisioning so that inherited and generational disadvantages are addressed; or should an educational market cater to the economic abilities of parents to choose schools?

Global Agendas and Education Markets

As school education in India is increasingly directed by international aid agencies and by international market forces, it is subject to agendas that seek to fit it into the new global economy and orientation. While ideas of inclusion (which challenge entrenched regional, class, caste, and gender differences) and need for improved administrative efficiency and monitoring are the contributions of such global directives, there are problems in the conceptualisation of 'quality' and in the overall restructuring of the system. For one, schools are increasingly seen as sites in which the global worker is to be produced, and literacy, numeracy, and 'minimum learning levels' are stipulated. Assessments and prescriptions by agencies such as the World Bank, which focus on education as delivering on 'human capital formation', value for money, and productivity of finances, etc., call for '...developing countries like India (to make) more use of private provision in the delivery of education' (Muralidharan and Sundararaman 2013: 24). Prescriptions like these override what should be the larger goals and objectives of education in enabling equality of opportunity for all. Such globalised agendas, drawn up on hegemonic economic rationale, further create distortions in the education system, thereby altering the public's perception of what is relevant or valid for them.[23] The state increasingly endorses these views and sees education as a sector in which the private sector or corporate groups have a significant role in all matters pertaining to education.

In fostering and legitimising school differentiation, the state becomes party to a process of reproducing a hierarchical society. Despite the state's rhetoric of 'inclusive growth' and inclusive development, the promotion and support of differentiated and graded schools belies the veracity of any formal statements of inclusion. Exhibiting exclusionary tendencies, such a differentiated schooling system clearly marks the mass versus the elite institutions, grades the range of schools that are available to the public, and also pits them against each other. This is reflected in the cases in which the stipulation of the RTE (2009) that 25 per cent of seats in private schools be reserved for children from economically disadvantaged families is increasingly being questioned by the management bodies of private schools. Or, in cases where it is implemented (by having to subscribe to the norms of the Act), there are widespread reports of resistance by teachers and parents, resulting in either high dropout rates of children or in their harassment and ill-treatment (Sarin and Gupta 2013).

Ideally, 'A democratic society must educate all educable children to be capable of participating in collectively shaping their society' (Gutman 1990: 12). Far from this, the differentiated schools in India act as filters, separating, segregating, and marking children with differential opportunities to education and life-chances. In denying both a level playing field and equality of educational outcomes, schools have become the sources of reproduced inequities. Subsequently, the failure to generate and sustain a collective orientation, and the growing differentiation of schools has several implications for children, the diverse societies in the country, and the nation.

Implications of 'School Differentiation'

Cultural pluralism, as the nation's palimpsest of an old civilisation melding into modernity, has been the bedrock of India's national fabric and has been fairly well-sustained by a inclusive policy that recognises and permits religious, linguistic, and regional differences.[24] For a nation with varied physio-geographic characteristics, 6,748 different types of communities,

780 languages,[25] and four major religions and multiple sects, a rigidly uniform system of schooling will not be viable or relevant. Yet, there have been no substantial efforts to recognise the plurality of life conditions, cultural preferences, and educational practices and, at the same time, provide for a foundation on which there can be equality of educational opportunity.

Shukla (1962), in a prescient essay, questioned whether the real plurality of the nation, based on cultural, religious, and linguistic variations, was represented in schools, and whether such real pluralism is sustained and reproduced by the absence of schooling. Contemporary trends indicate that we must reckon with such a contradiction as the wide variations in schooling seem to segregate and enhance the class and cultural divides among people. Much of this is reminiscent of what Ambedkar (1987[1936]) had elaborated—the specificity of inequality in caste society was one of 'graded inequality', where infinite divisions and separations existed between groups. In the context of the new alterations in the economy and polity, such 'graded inequality' is also manifesting in education. Changing social structures facilitate or encourage variations in school choice—this is visible not only in the urban areas where the growth of a 'new middle class'[26] has been apparent, but also in the rural areas. It is evident in the increasingly dual economies (subsistence and commercial) of the rural belts—the working poor are forced to rely on government schools while the smaller proportion of the landed and the newly emerging middle classes[27] are now seeking private education. It is a similar story in the urban areas, where a range of private schools is catering to the complex and varying urban middle classes (Tooley and Dixon 2005), while the number and provisioning of schools for those residing in urban poverty/slum areas has shrunk. More glaring are the differences created by the newly globalising economy, which enables a small proportion of families to have access to what are considered world-class schools, while state provisioning for the working class continues to be limited in all aspects. A result of such variations is evident in the sharp economic differences in the costs and facilities of different schools. For example, the annual fee paid (approximately Rs 5,00,000–6,00,000 per annum in 2020 and going upto Rs 10,00,000 in some schools[28]) for a child to attend an international school is often more than the annual education budget of a panchayat or village school catering to about 250 children living in the vicinity of that school.

Encapsulating and representing such separatism and insularity, each of the different types of schools also acts as a different processual site. Mass government schools are part of the developmentalist, welfare regimes of governmentality,[29] where minimum levels of feeding, clothing, and provisioning take place. Here, a politics of legitimation is evident as the state seeks to assert its role as the provisioner of the social sector that has value only as an electoral base. Private schools that cater to the middle classes act as sites where the ambitions and aspirations of parents are catered to and sought to be realised. Elite schools act primarily as couriers/carriers of symbolic and social capital, which can further enable students to capitalise on their access to economic capital and hence facilitate increased capital accumulation. Here the focus is on sustaining and reproducing the privileges of elite children, and in making possible the reproduction of privilege through the social and cultural capital that education and specific schools as institutions can provide. Such differentiated schools and the subsequent schooling system have, in turn, created a further divide of caste, class, and gender differences. It is not unusual to now come across villages in which the local government school caters primarily to the poorest, the low-ranked caste groups, and to girls, while upper-caste children and many boys from even the labouring poor are in private schools.[30]

In catering to these economic and social priorities, such a differentiated schooling system denies the coming together of children from varied backgrounds, and violates the very possibility of schools acting as the foundation on which shared sensibilities and a sense of belonging could be developed. Subsequently, schools have become part of the larger system of graded institutions that overtly and covertly mark individuals with differentiated skills, knowledge, and abilities. As sources of the range of capital (Bourdieu 2010), economic, social, and cultural, which later determine the access to further economic capital, a differentiated schooling system forms the bedrock on which India's inequality, hierarchy, and dis/advantages are reproduced.

Employment and School Differentiation

In some ways, similar to the 'correspondence principle' articulated by Bowles and Gintis (1976), school differentiation plays out the triangular relationship between family or household abilities, the school, and the job market. Mass education, especially that provided by the government schools, locates children primarily in labour pools or as potential labour, since dropout or elimination rates are high (only about 40 per cent of children make it up to high school, and only 11 per cent of the cohort between the ages of 18–24 years is in higher education [GoI 2018]). Largely, the ability of most of the graduates from government schools to compete at higher levels is negated. On the other hand, elite education channels children into a tunnel of academic high achievement aimed at the realisation of select and dominant career choices. In the context of a booming, urban, and globalising economy, the results of such school differentiation are also manifesting in various problems of employment allocation. School and early educational background influence and impact economic opportunity; this is elaborated by Anirudh Krishna's study (2014). The study indicates that students from rural areas and rural schools (and therefore, a majority from government schools) are particularly disadvantaged, have significantly less access to the new range of higher educational institutions and, subsequently, to the new employment opportunities in the global economy. This foundational disadvantage in schools manifests as problems at several levels. For one, those who do make it into higher education (especially through positive discrimination or the reservation system) find themselves unable to match the academic competence of those from more privileged schools and educated families, which then leads to their being labelled and identified as 'weak students'. As sociologist Satish Deshpande[31] has elaborated, the oversight of these foundational disadvantages that most rural and/or SC/ST students face leads to the construction and assigning of blame to the reservation system. These oversights largely account for the range of blaming that universities invoke to excuse their own inability to address issues of learning and quality. The continuation of such disadvantages even after graduation then leads to the peculiar situation of a large number of graduates remaining unemployed, even while the booming urban market with its focus on the new service and high-tech sector is unable to find adequate numbers of trained and employable youth to fill positions. As a result, millions of youth are cast aside as being useless for the urban, global employment market. Science institutions constantly bemoan the dearth of students in the basic sciences, even as a significant proportion, primarily from the government schooling system, is unable to pass the Standard X exams. Jean Anyon's observation, that 'an unequal distribution of knowledge and work dispositions in school could be said not merely to reproduce social inequality, but to exacerbate it by supporting a bifurcation of incomes and class structure' (2006: 37), is fully relevant here, and reflects the extent to which school differentiation forms the foundational and institutional bases of professional and class exclusion in India.

Democratic Deficits

The potential of schools to play a key role in democratising society, and then sustaining democracy as a larger socio-political entity on a national level, has been elaborated on by several scholars (Apple 1993; Dewey 1916; Gutman 1987). But in a hierarchical and differentiated schooling system, the very possibility of enabling children to engage in a collective shaping of their society is challenged, and the possibility of generating a democratic culture and of creating social resemblances, which in turn can foster or support democracy, is lost. If common schools can and do act as shared sites that facilitate shared experiences and bridge generational social, religious, and economic divides, then the loss of these schools is also detrimental for the very social fabric of any community. In 2000, I documented one village in Kerala with a population of about a 1,000-plus households where children attended seven different types of schools, which ranged from the panchayat-run government school to the Mata Amritanandamayi Matha-run English-medium CBSE school.[32] The separation of the village children into different schools marked a contrast to the earlier pattern where the older generation of parents and grandparents had attended one single government school, and had developed a sense of community and of belonging among themselves. However, the new diversity of schools, reflecting the increasing social and economic fragmentation, not only enhances the social and economic divides among village members, but also erodes any possibility of a sense of belonging and a shared sociality among the children of the current generation. The challenges that such exclusive schools, which become homogenous in their student body, pose to the very educational orientation has been elaborated by Krishna Kumar. If education is about the recognition of the diversity and meanings of life and of learning ways to understand and relate to these, then a homogenous school body 'negates the very idea of the relatedness of human beings' (Kumar 1992: 49), and makes students insular and indifferent.

Although the Kothari Commission[33] had recommended the establishment of 'common schools' as a way to bring about equality of education opportunity, the state's commitment to enforcing or realising this has been largely absent. Permitting a proliferation of schools and an education market has negated the possibility of fostering either a shared 'public' or associating democracy with the larger fabric of society, and of allowing a democratic ethos to be embedded within educational institutions and their functioning. This largely accounts for the widespread 'democratic deficits' that some scholars have spoken about, and which are glaring in the everyday private and public lives of Indians. This is pertinent, as the structural basis of this highly differentiated schooling system is responsible for the persistence of inequities, and the widespread and complex problems that arise from the denial of equality of educational opportunity to all. Far from ensuring equality of educational opportunity and educational outcomes, the expanding educational market erodes the possibility of inclusion and pluralism. Instead, we are witness to the rise of enhanced separatism, in which the school is the key marker.

Schools and the Deepening of Democracy

At a time when decentralised administration is being promoted and the possibility of making elected representatives accountable to the people is being enhanced, school differentiation becomes counter-productive to the new political structures that can ensure the participation of disadvantaged groups, and therefore the deepening of democratic processes. New directives which stipulate the involvement of 'community' or parents in the administration of government schools are rendered vacuous or have become unviable, as the most advantaged parents have their children in private schools, leaving only the most disadvantaged parents to relate to the school administration. The subsequent inability of low-ranked caste groups and economically disadvantaged families to hold teachers and/or the education administration accountable to them has also led to hamlets and villages with predominantly lower-caste groups having lower functioning or ineffective schools.[34] Similarly, Manjrekar (n.d.) describes a government school located in a Muslim locality in the heart of Baroda city, which is subject to deliberate administrative and state neglect, as representing the inability of marginalised communities to command and receive what is legitimately due to them.

The impact of such school differentiation has also meant that the community of parents or the larger public is unable to come together to address the structural inadequacies of the system. Instead, problems related to schools and schooling are no longer shared through a single school or system, and are instead experienced by different groups or classes of people in different ways. Similarly, if problems are addressed at all, it is done so in different and individualised ways. Although parents rue the decline in the quality of education in government and private schools or complain about the myriad problems that they or their children experience, their failure or inability to collectively engage with problems has become one of the reasons for the continued crisis in the quality, orientation, and impact of schooling.

Impact of School Differentiation on the Lives of Children

Another fallout of school differentiation is to be observed at the level of its impact on the lives of children. Even as government schools lack adequate opportunities to engage children and equip them with competent skills and knowledge, private and elite schools are increasingly overloading their students. The excessive emphasis on academic performance by middle- and upper-class adolescents largely accounts for the high suicide rate among them. This split in expectations—high and excessive expectation among and of children from the middle and upper classes, and no expectation at all (and hence overlooking the potential talent pool) of the lower and working classes— manifests in different ways in the job market. It is no wonder that this double jeopardy (the poorer you are, the lower the quality of education, and hence the less equality of educational opportunities) that the education system bestows on poor and disadvantaged children has met with criticism and even cynicism about education among parents. This is highlighted in Jeffrey et al's (2007) study, wherein low-ranked caste men who have been 'educated' but not absorbed into formal employment, and who have eschewed the manual and agricultural labour of their parents, become a burden on their families and the society. Through hanging out with their peers and being unemployed, they induce among the older residents and parents an anti-education attitude, which questions the very worth of such formal education.

The impact of a hierarchical differentiation of schools, which marks children as differentiated citizens without a common and shared ethos, has also been visible in upper-caste students' insensitive reactions and violent hostility towards policies of positive discrimination or the policy of reservations.[35] The failure of schools to cultivate a sense of empathy and sharing indicates the extent to which the differentiated educational system has reinforced a lack of commitment to creating not only an equitable society, but has also legitimised and strengthened the idea that society can be 'acceptably unequal' (Whitty 1998: 94).

The children in each of these schools occupy different and graded positions as citizens. Poor and disadvantaged children are treated as mass supplicants and are subject to a poor quality regime of education. The middle classes are offered a competitive educational regime that seeks to fit them into urban, professional occupational structures. For elite children, there is a platter of possibilities—personalised, customised, and even designer education. Do privileged schools generate and enable creative and innovative abilities among their students? That this may not be so is an issue that Krishna Kumar (1992) has flagged, by highlighting the fact that the alumni of such schools have not contributed to any significant process or development in the nation. Although discussions and reviews pertaining to this are rare, some data indicate such a tendency. For example, Upadhya's study (2007) on the social background of India's Information Technology (IT) entrepreneurs indicates that many of them, who contribute significantly to the economy and to generating employment, are from municipal or government schools, thereby indicating that elite schools may not necessarily provide the foundation for entrepreneurship and innovation.

While the most significant and visible aspect of such differentiation is the failure to provide equal opportunities and equality of educational outcomes, the long-term impact is also at the level of a national culture. If, in the Nehruvian imaginary, the nation was to be a palimpsest of plural societies in which different cultures could be intertwined and the nation could absorb this over generations, the current global imaginary focuses on reproducing different and unequal societies that are enfolded into exclusionary enclaves and bounded by economic and institutional differences. In the failure to generate a comprehensive policy for a common schooling system or to support processes that would enable a diversity of schools (with variations in language and organisation/functioning), but with similar standards (in funding, infrastructure, and content) to arrive at a common platform, schools in India have become the key sources through which inequities are being reproduced. In promoting, both consciously and by default, schools that are differentiated by class, region, religion, language, and standards, the state is abdicating its primary role in fostering education for democracy and realising a democratic society which can in turn sustain a democratic polity. Although Gandhi and Tagore[36] elaborated on new forms of education that could overcome the limitations of existing forms of formal education, their vision and endeavours have been neither realised nor sustained. Instead, as a post-colonial democratic nation, Dewey's (1916) stipulation of the links between education and democracy also seems a distant and deliberately ignored perspective. Instead, what we are witness to is increasing hierarchical differentiation, in which exclusion and further distanciation between citizens is being created. If schools must bear the mandate that to 'be just and equal, (they) must contribute to the advantage of the least advantaged', and if 'Education...must play a part with other economic and social institutions in redistributing cultural and economic capital more justly' (Arnot 2006: 24), then India's schooling system is a long way away from this ideal goal.

If hierarchical school differentiation and its impact on individuals, society, and the nation are to be addressed, then there is a need to take stock and assess the real significance and role of schools. Speaking in 1932 after his visit to schools in the then Soviet Union, the educationist George Counts (1996 [1932]) called on educationists to 'Dare Schools to Challenge the Social Order'. He spoke of going beyond the then prevailing ideas of progressive education and observed the strong association of democracy with schools. Calling on educationists to see schools as sites that would enable its graduates to become agents of micro and macro changes, he stressed the possibility of working towards the establishment of just and equitable social orders. If we were to keep this in mind and make it the key role of school education to challenge existing iniquitous social orders, then the first principle is to challenge the very differentiation of schools. Only a shared and equitable education system can make possible the structures and agencies that can tackle the challenge of multiple inequities.

That this is an ideal which will face insurmountable challenges is evident in the content and orientation of the two PILs on elementary education, discussed at the beginning of this chapter. These PILs indicate the extent to which education, especially at the elementary stage, is now largely delinked from a commitment to social justice, wherein

> education is not just about the equalisation of opportunity in classical liberal social theory, about a hypothetical freedom to 'compete' for unequal outcomes and differential successes, but potentially about the opening up of access to valued forms of cultural practice and knowledge to students from communities that historically had been excluded from capital, status and power (Luke 2000: 138).

If such possibilities have been largely eroded, then the growing education differentiation is not reflective of the cultural pluralism of the nation, but is instead a conduit for the reproduction of the multiple forms of separatism that are already hallmarks of the larger Indian society and its cultures. Located in different socio-economic structures and focused on reproducing those very structures, schools in India are institutions that only formally espouse ideals of democracy, modernity, and progress. In reality, they are institutionalised conduits that largely reproduce an inegalitarian society.

NOTES

1. For details of the PIL by Ravindra Talpe and Uday Warunjikar, see *The New Indian Express* (2017).
2. The case against the RTE 2009 has witnessed several twists and turns. In 2012, the Supreme Court dismissed the case by the Society of Unaided Private Schools of Rajasthan and upheld the validity of the RTE 2009; see https://www.right-to-education.org/sites/right-to-education.org/files/resource-attachments/India%20Supreme%20Court%2C%20Society%20for%20Unaided%20Private%20Schools%20v%20India%2C%202012.pdf However, another case relates to the questioning of the RTE 2009 for minority (religious and linguistic) institutions. This is the writ petition filed by the Pramati Educational and Cultural Trust & Others, where the judgment (6 May 2014) indicates that the

Supreme Court upholds the rights of such minority institutions to *not* implement the quota for children from economically disadvantaged groups. See https://indiankanoon.org/doc/32468867/ (accessed August 2022).

3. Data on size, types, and trends in India's schooling system is not easily accessible. Various reports for different periods indicate growth, but analytical data that makes interlinkages between elementary, secondary, and higher education is rare. The Ministry of Human Resource Development's (MHRD) annual reports provide some data, but the focus is on showcasing achievements, and hence lack a critical and authentic review. NUEPA's DISE (District Information System for Education) reports and analytical studies provide data, but aggregated data for all levels and types of schools is not available.
4. Bourdieu's wide range of writings has elaborated on the idea of 'capital', both social and cultural. For a contextualised exegesis on social and cultural capital in the context of education, see his writings in the collected works (Bourdieu 2010).
5. According to the Government of India (2018) data, there are 11,02,783 government schools.
6. See a range of review reports: Annual Status of Education Reports (ASER 2014, 2017), Human Rights Watch (2014), NUEPA (2011, 2014).
7. For an excellent overview of the differences between public and private schools in India, see Jain (2018).
8. British Public Schools are schools which can charge fees and recruit students, irrespective of the students' location, religious background, and parental occupation.
9. Ekal Vidyalayas are run by the Ekal Abhiyan Trust, an umbrella organisation that manages several education programmes and activities to promote education in rural tribal belts. See: https://www.ekal.org/in/about-ekal-india.
10. Data from the 'Kendriya Vidyalaya' website (www.kvsangathan.nic.in).
11. Many KVs are located in green field public sector organisations such as steel factories, nuclear sites, defence centres, and so on. A few examples are HAL, BEL, BHEL, Atomic Energy sites in Rourkela, Asansol, etc; also in metropolitan areas where there are large factories such as BHEL in Bengaluru.
12. The term 'common schools' refers to integrated, neighbourhood-based, and government-managed schools recommended by several

policy reports (for example, the Kothari Commission) and by education rights activists.

13. 'Magnet' schools are used to refer to schools that are set up to attract high performing children. These are not meant to be for the elite but are projected as 'elite' or better schools.
14. For an overall review of ashramshalas, see the report by P. Veerabhadranaika et al. (2012).
15. See Education World (2007) for a review of the KGBVs.
16. Madrassas are meant primarily for disseminating the reading and learning of the Quran and are mostly run by Mosques and Islamic religious organisations. For details on madrassas, see Yoginder Sikand (2005). Pathshalas used to be established by the rural elite to cater to the learning needs of their children and those of their caste groups.
17. A representative case of such new 'religion-based' schools is the establishment of 'gurukuls', some of which call themselves 'Gurukul International Schools', and in which Sanskrit and Vedic education are taught along with computer and other technical skills. An example of an expanding 'Gurukul International School' network is the schools run by the Swaminarayan sect.
18. For example, what are considered elite residential schools, such as the Lawrence Schools in Lovedale (Tamil Nadu) and at Sanawar (Himachal Pradesh), are managed by the MHRD, but have links to the Department of Defence as they cater to the children of Defence officers.
19. Contentious issues include not only medium of education, but also textbooks and their content. For example, what is referred to as the 'saffronisation of school texts' relates to the Hinduisation of school materials by right-wing Hindutva forces, which seek to present and consolidate a simplistic and romanticised version of a glorious Hindu past.
20. For an earlier and comprehensive elaboration of the implications of such cultural dissonance that results from English as a medium of instruction, see Kumar (1996).
21. For example, advertisements for new international schools describe and promote the schools in terms of their infrastructure, which include air-conditioned classrooms, mini-golf courses, Olympic-sized swimming pools, international cuisine, etc. Such advertisements are also building on the idea that parents seek to prepare their children for a global lifestyle.

22. Education service providers include a number of companies and consultants who design, develop, advise, and even manage schools for a fee. Advertisements indicate that such education service providers claim to provide not only teacher training, development of curricula and content, pedagogies, etc., but also software packages for monitoring and administration, and deliver extra-curricular activities and support to private schools. In addition, providing technical support for school infrastructure and academic inputs have also drawn in a number of players.
23. The stipulation of minimum learning levels at the national level has focused on formal and academic learning at an early stage of children's lives, and largely overlooks the need for elementary education to have a comprehensive approach to learning and include the holistic well-being of children.
24. For an overview of India's cultural pluralism that constituted the bases of a new nation, see Khilnani (1997).
25. See the People of India project by the Anthropological Survey of India (Singh 1992) for details on the variations in communities. For recent data on language variations, see data on 'The People's Linguistic Survey of India' , available at peopleslinguisticsurvey.org (accessed July 2021).
26. For a comprehensive review of the growth of the new middle classes, see Fernandes and Heller (2006).
27. For details of rural variations and the growth of new economies, see Vasavi (2012).
28. In US dollars, the annual fee is about 8,000–10,000 per year in the international schools, or an average of Rs 6,00,000 per year per child, while the average expenditure per village school for about 200 students would be much less than that.
29. I draw on the term 'welfare governmentality' from Kalyan Sanyal (2007), where he refers to the forms of welfare provisioning by the state that seeks to govern people and political dissent.
30. For data and studies that highlight this variation in the caste and gender composition of schools, see Majumdar and Mooij (2011).
31. From his lecture, 'Beyond Access: Challenges in Higher Education', delivered as the K.R. Narayanan Memorial Lecture at the Centre for Research and Education in Social Transformation (CREST), Kozhikode, 15 March 2014.
32. The seven different types of schools which the children in this coastal village in north Kerala attended included the following five which

were located within the panchayat area: (*i*) Local panchayat school; (*ii*) A private school with Malayalam as medium of instruction; (*iii*) Convent school run by the sisters of a Catholic church; (*iv*) A school run by a Muslim charitable group; (*v*) A private school affiliated to the CBSE board. In addition, children attended two other schools which were in the nearest town, the school run by the Mata Amritanandamayi organisation, and an expensive private school which offered English- medium education and was affiliated to the CBSE board (New Delhi).

33. Kothari Commission or the Education Commission of 1964–1966 (Government of India 1966).
34. See details of such caste-based differences in schools in the reports by the National Institute of Advanced Studies (2001a, 2001b, 2001c).
35 The 'Anti-Mandal' agitation of 1990 was led primarily by upper-caste and upper-class students who resented the reservation policy for disadvantaged and low-ranked caste group students.
36. Gandhi elaborated on an alternative basic educational system called 'Nai Talim' (New Learning), in which the 'head, heart, and hand' were to be integrated, and in which vocational training and skills were to be encouraged. The Nai Talim schools and system have subsequently been abandoned, and only a few select schools are being run by individuals. Rabindranath Tagore's educational endeavours focused on recognising the individual and creative dimensions of every individual, and much of this was articulated and even institutionalised in Shantiniketan,which is a university town today (established by his father, Devendranath Tagore, and expanded by Tagore later). This has also been largely neglected, and Visva Bharati University at Shantiniketan today stands embroiled in issues of maladministration.

IV

CONUNDRUMS OF 'COMMUNITY'

Participation in India's Elementary Education System

In her book *The Politics of Gender, Community, and Modernity: Essays on Education in India* (2007), historian Nita Kumar calls attention to the historic moments in which epistemological shifts were induced by the British in their colonial administration of India's education. She singles out the post-1850s, during which three new and key elements in education were introduced. These were: (*i*) the introduction of new technologies, spaces, and buildings; (*ii*) inserting new philosophies; and (*iii*) investing the education system with additional powers, primarily according centrality to the government in education. As Kumar notes, all these led to shifts away from the family, caste, and community's engagement with education and towards the centrality of the state.

In a similar vein, I would like to locate the contemporary predicament of mass elementary education in India in the post-1993 phase, in which a reversal, after nearly 140 years, is underway. Here, the role of 'communities', especially through the structures of decentralised administration of elementary education, has gained currency and is mediated by the state, even as privatisation is promoted. But the realisation of such interlinkages, in which members of communities are to play proactive roles and gain control over schools, is fraught with several tensions. For one, the according of legitimacy and roles in elementary education to parents and community members by the state, and even the World Bank, creates issues which concern the very conditions and definitions of communities, their ability to engage in education, and the challenges they face in engaging with or reclaiming their role in education. Second, the school as an institution, its significance, meaning, and linkage to the community itself, has changed substantially. Therefore, the process and realigning of links between community and school must be located both within the national-level macro-structural characteristics of the education system, and in the localised micro-specificities and processes in which the new alignment and orientation are sought to be realised. These new shifts in the management of education have implications for the power relations between the state and the people, and are also significant in the history and sociology of elementary education, now in its mass phase in India.

This chapter reviews these issues in three separate sections. The first section unpacks the meanings (and thereby the implications and expectations) of the term 'communities' embedded in the policy documents pertaining to elementary education, the problems of such representation, and some trends in the conditions of communities in contemporary India. The second section is a review of the actual trends in the implementation of programmes to enhance community participation and administration of schools in various states of India, and the key lessons that can be discerned from them. The third and concluding section focuses on raising some socio-political issues related to community-administered or community-based elementary education.

Constructions of 'Community' in Policy and Programme Papers

Although periodic expressions of intent to establish local self-governments[1] have made their rounds since 1950, the first coherent stipulation for education decentralisation can be credited to the passing of the 73rd and 74th Constitutional Amendments, related to the establishment of decentralised administration or local self-government (Panchayat Raj) Acts of 1993. The Central Advisory Board of Education (CABE 1993) recommended the setting up of Village Education Committees (VECs) at village school levels, and Education Committees (ECs) at the block levels as part of the panchayat system itself (Raina 2002). Subsequently, key national programmes such as the District Primary Education Programme (DPEP) of 1994, and the 'Sarva Shiksha Abhiyan' (Education for All) of 2001, which have been supported by international agencies, and the 93rd Constitutional Amendment Bill which evolved into the 86th Constitution Amendment Act (Right to Elementary Education), have reiterated the need for decentralised, community-based structures so as to enhance the efficiency and accountability of elementary education administration.

These endeavours draw on earlier and long-standing concepts and ideas, on the basis of which international development programmes have been designed to include popular participation and community contribution. The focus on 'community' has often been associated with attempts to overcome the limitations of centralisation, bureaucratisation, and excessive regulation, and/or as ways to stall subversive activities against state or capitalist agendas (Midgley 1986). The idea of facilitating community participation in decision-making and in the allocation of benefits has been premised on the belief that such structuring would lead to the 'involvement of the poor in the life of the community so that it is able to act democratically in its dealings with the outside world' (ibid.: 26). In summary, community-oriented policies and programmes have sought to see community-focused work as both the means and the end of democratic processes, as strategies that are to be broad-based and inclusive, and as ways to enhance the accountability of larger administrative or delivery structures and mechanisms. But as Jock Young (2007) has elaborated, the idea and promotion of 'community' itself needs to be interrogated, as there is a tendency to obfuscate the details and particularities of communities, and assign organic characteristics to them.

As the now rich literature on 'communities' has highlighted, the term is loaded both philosophically and sociologically. The communitarian roots of the term underscore the reference and call towards integrationist and participatory dimensions (Benhabib 1992). In gaining sociological currency, the term has been a referent to an idealised social world of small, primary relationships, which are 'characterised by a high degree of personal intimacy, emotional depth, moral commitment, social cohesion and continuity in time' (Nisbet 1967: 47–48). In the field of education, these constructions of community have been reinforced by both popular and academic ideas that have considered community the most important site of fostering education. A dialogical relationship in which communities support schools, which in turn foster good communities, has been the bedrock of many American education policies (Gardner 1996). Leading scholars and educationists such as Paulo Freire (1999) have endorsed community-based education so as to question dominant powers, and to also facilitate democratic processes in newly developing countries.

Most policy documents in India draw on these ideas of 'community' as both an organisation and society, and expectations of their roles in education. Idealised images of settlement-based communities are invoked, or are embedded in policy documents, and many policy-makers assign a range of responsibilities and goals to 'communities'. In addition to these ideas, embedded unconsciously in the texts and documents[2] are a range of concepts and ideas about what 'communities' are and should be. Unpacking these terms, processes, and structures by which administrative measures may/may not have been successful in promoting the role of communities in elementary education will enable us to assess the promise inherent in, and the problems of, pursuing such policies.

A key source of construction of the community in most of the policies and programmes related to community-school linkages has been the assumption of the rural context of communities. Given India's history of being a predominantly rural civilisation and nation, such a construction is understandable. However, in limiting this conceptualisation to the rural and predominantly agrarian context, the realities and needs of urban citizens, especially of the urban poor and working class who also rely on government schools, are overlooked. A key result of this is that policies and programmes have also then failed to envisage what structures and which processes can facilitate urban citizens to relate to schools under such conditions. Consequently, issues of education exclusion, elimination, and inadequate provisioning of facilities and their management in urban poverty areas have become more problematic than even in the rural areas.[3]

In this aligning of communities to rural areas, two other dominant ideas have been influential. One is that of an overarching understanding and representation of community in communitarian ideas. In all these contexts, the community is associated with persons living in a bounded space, having similar identities, and enjoying a sense of solidarity. All communities are also expected to have continuity, cohesion, boundedness, and adherence to tradition. Much of this draws from the larger orientation to ideas of communities. Second, as Upadhya elaborates, the typical construct of a community in India is that of a 'substantialised, cultural, and essentialised notion' (2001: 52), which has then become established and commonsensical in India. Most policy and programme documents pertaining to promoting the role and contributions of the community in elementary administration also reproduce these ideas.

Drawing on such conceptualisations, there are four different assumptions about 'communities' embedded in these documents. One of these refers to Gandhi's ideas and postulates of what a community is, and the role it could play in the life of the nation. Drawing on a near romanticised idea, the community, and primarily the rural community, for Gandhi was a harmonious, integral institution that functioned to serve the needs of all. For him, the community was an inherent moral order that was self-sufficient and non-exploitative. In the imaginings of a new, postcolonial and *Swaraj* (independent) order, the community was to be the site of economy, polity, and sociality. And although many of Gandhi's directives for the new economy were not followed, the idea of decentralised administration and the role of the community in it are drawn, albeit vicariously, from him. While the overriding tone of most government documents resonate with Gandhian ideals and expectations, in many ways they overlook the real conditions of village communities as sites of caste-based conflict, tensions, and exclusion. Although Ambedkar's critique of this construction of the village as a harmonious whole was not taken seriously,[4] it is only recently that studies and representations of village communities have sought to highlight the intense fragmentation and contestations apparent in these communities.

Continuing such an orientation, most of the documents that invoke the role of elected representatives draw on the implicit idea that decentralised bodies will bear in mind the common good of the larger community and work in terms of a 'trusteeship'. Such community leaders are expected to discharge their responsibilities and address the range of problems that schools face. In ascribing such characteristics, what is often overlooked is the class position of leaders: leaders may not share the same life conditions as that of the larger community, especially the disadvantaged, who they may also represent. A common problem is the fact that given the class variations between leaders and the others, often, the children of the leaders do not attend the government school, and leaders fail to take schools and school-related issues seriously or accord them the significance that they deserve.

Another source for ideas of 'community' was the influential Community Development Programme of the 1950s, which has left an imprint on policy approaches and programmes. Conceptualised primarily by American aid specialists, such a focus on community overlooked the reality of the hierarchical and graded inequality of the average Indian village, and expected economic growth to be initiated through technological alterations in the agrarian economy. While reviews of the Community Development Programme and its projects have indicated the extent to which this has been problematic (Jena 2007), the fact that much of the benefits were garnered by either the elite of the identified settlements or communities or by bureaucrats and administrators (Midgley 1986) continues to be overlooked even in recent policy documents for elementary education. The continuing hold of such ideas has been visible in the conceptualisation of the VECs, and other similar structures such as the ECs or 'Shiksha Samitis'. In assigning roles of responsibility to such structures, policy-makers have often overlooked the extent to which these structures/organisations, or the members within such organisations, embedded as they are within localised structures of hierarchy and socio-economic and cultural differences, may not be able to address problems of access, exclusion, and institution-building (Subramanian 2000).

The policy documents and programmes also overlook the fact that not all communities have equal social capital[5] and capabilities. The type and range of symbols that constitute a community (Cohen 1985) have implications for the ways in which the community handles or deals with external institutions and agencies. Overlooking these characteristics, which underlie most of these policy documents, means that administrators often regard communities, and expect them to act, as civil society organisations. As a result, there is a presumption that such structures, or the members of the communities who are engaged in such administrative structures, will have associational characteristics, which will enhance their sociability and allow them to lend themselves to achieving collective goals (Chandhoke 2003). In the context of elementary education administration, one such collective goal assigned to the community is for it to deploy its collective agency towards enhancing the individual accountability of teachers to the community. The extent to which this is feasible is linked to the varied constitutions and orientations of the different communities, and to the highly varied linkages between communities and schools. Settlements and, therefore, communities with upper-caste groups, can command better schools and teachers, in contrast to the settlements and communities of low-ranked caste groups, which are often allocated inadequate funds and lower-skilled teachers. Adding to this is the fact that communities have differential abilities to engage with formal structures and procedures. Marginalised and non-literate communities are far less equipped with the power to challenge these biases in the allocation of funds, and in enforcing the education administration to address issues of dysfunctional schools, and the problem of errant teachers. Schools of tribal (Adivasi) and marginal communities such as those of the Scheduled Castes, and even some Backward Classes, which are typically in less accessible areas and considered punitive posts for teachers, tend to face these problems. Even in contexts where community-based structures are formed, the inability of community members to engage with upper-caste teachers and the culture of political and social subordination limit the ability of marginalised persons and groups, including women, to challenge such discrimination and/or violations of norms.

Documents and policy papers also envisage a simplistic relationship between communities and the school, where the school as an institution is located within the realm of the community. However, in reality the community–school relationship is shaped by larger political and economic structures, of which the community and school are only a part. As a result, the real relationship or the forms of engagement between the two are defined by the power relations, the culture, and the political, economic, and socio-economic matrix within which communities interact with schools. These relationships in India are very unlike those in the West, such as in the US, where community administration of schools is based on the rights and abilities of communities (as represented by members of a settlement or a residential zone) to control schools. In such contexts, these administrative structures invoke questions of the 'zone of tolerance' (McGivney and Moynihan 1972), where the community permits, tolerates, or supports the leadership, abilities, inputs, etc., of the school authorities (who are accountable to them). In contrast, in India, the recent introduction of decentralised administration, both in invoking the general rights of communities to be involved in schools and in the recent politically legitimised domains (such as Panchayati Raj institutions), is not based on such an assumption (of communities being able to administer elementary education on their own). Instead, given that community-school linkages are sought to be forged for government and mass elementary schools, which are accessed by the marginalised, such assumptions of the possible power the community holds over the school are questionable. In fact, a reverse vertical linkage can be identified where, in a typical community of predominantly non-literate adults, the teacher, as a government employee, enjoys more cultural and real power over the disadvantaged community.

The Contemporary Predicament of Rural Communities

While the above ideas and expectations of community-school relations are embedded within most official documents, we need to delineate and understand the contemporary predicament of rural communities,[6] and therefore that of the sociological reality of Indian communities. Conceptions of communities need to factor in complexities that should include not only a micro politico-economic perspective, in which communities are understood as 'political associations formed through processes of political and cultural creation and imagination' (Li 1996: 508), but also one in which communities are seen as historico-cultural entities with specific social characteristics. Such characteristics include the shared understandings that members of communities have amongst themselves, and the specific organisational structure of these communities (Agarwal 1999). This is central, as government programmes have tended to form, identify, and redefine 'communities' based on the 'constructed notions of local autonomy and resource sovereignty' (Sivaramakrishnan 2000: 433).

In addition, as several studies have detailed,[7] the impact of economic liberalisation has enhanced economic and social differentiation, leading to complex shifts in intra- and inter-caste relationships. Despite sharp regional and state variations in trends, some broad generalisations are tenable. In rural areas, the landed 'proprietary classes' (Bardhan 1984; Vasavi 2018), especially those in the Green Revolution belt, have emerged as 'farmer entrepreneurs' with close ties to the growing urban trade and economy. Consolidating their economic and social positions, they continue to be not only the dominant caste groups, but also the political elites in the altering and varied political structures of different states. Middle-ranking artisan and service caste groups, including those classified in official nomenclature as 'Other Backward Classes' (OBCs), have been subject to processes of displacement, and are compelled to resort to migration, either permanent or seasonal, so as to eke out livelihoods. Large sections of wage workers and the landless, who are predominantly from the low-ranked caste groups, continue to be retained in conditions of non-free, non-capitalist structures and relations of production.

In the peri-urban belts in the vicinity of the large and growing metropolises, there are trends of a significant proportion of people earning their livelihood from non-agricultural employment and services (Nayyar and Sharma 2005). In this context, there is a rising class of persons who, as employees of the government sector or of the urban and service sectors, are emerging as a new class of intermediaries, with links and relationships to the rural. For the working poor of the urban metropolitan areas, the cities no longer offer the space and possibility of permanent settlement, and hence they must resort to seasonal and periodic migration to sustain themselves (Kundu 2006).

All of these have implications for the meaning and significance of 'community' and its linkages to schools. For such trends indicate that the contemporary sociological reality of communities in India is not of a neat identification with caste, village, or religious groups alone. Instead, what are observable are complex conditions wherein articulations between local, micro-conditions, and macro-factors have wrought involutions, so much so that it is appropriate to understand such conditions as reflecting aspects of 'post, post-colonial transformation' (Tanabe 2007: 559) of societies in India. Such transformations include not only the ongoing engagements between traditional and modern cultures, but also the formation and presence of civil, political, and moral societies.[8] Located within different socio-political worlds, persons and groups are then engaged in transacting and negotiating through these various societies, and their associated norms and values.

These complex socio-economic and political configurations within which people are located also influence the type of relationships that community members have with schools. Given the variation in the socio-economic and political status of communities/settlements, the relationship between community members and schools can be of at least three types, based on the power equations between them. Relevant for a majority of cases and situations are conditions where the community/settlement engages with the school as an institution of the new economic and political realm. In such cases, schools deploy normalising techniques (that is, methods and processes which become accepted as legitimate and inevitable) and subject the members of the community/settlement to the rules and norms of governmentality. Here, typically, the members of the community submit to the processes and demands made by the school. In a second condition, communities can seek to claim schools into their own localised realm of politics and economics. Subsequently, members may deploy strategies to access the goods and services available through the school, or seek to make decisions and the distribution of funds and jobs a part of their or their leaders' strategies of power, status, maintenance, or politics. Cases of communities thwarting and distorting rules related to the use and allocation of funds, the recruitment of personnel, and inter-caste commensality during midday meals are examples.

The third type of relationship may be discernible in cases where schools deploy and implement rules of governmentality, without sensitivity to the problems faced by members of the community. The community responds not with open defiance, but resorts to forms of resistance in which rules are sought to be subverted. Tribal (Adivasi) communities who are compelled to enrol their children into residential schools, but who send their children to the day school instead and continue to keep them home at night, the high rates of absenteeism during harvesting and festivals, the withdrawal of children during exams, etc., are all cases in point.

Based on the variations in the economic and social positions and conditions of communities, there is also a sharp variation in awareness and access to information and knowledge about new rules, laws, and institutions. Banerjee et al.'s (2007) study of 280 villages in Uttar Pradesh indicates that as many as 92 per cent of the people did not know about the VEC, and general participation in the new decentralised mechanisms was poor. As the authors note, 'overall, participation (at individual and collective level) in the activities to improve school functioning or strengthening learning is negligible' (ibid.: 1369). Although awareness-building and training programmes have been suggested, and were to be part of the implementation of even the Sarva Shiksha Abhiyan, there have been variations in the forms in which these trainings have been conducted. While some states draw on the strength of localised and periodic training and orientation, in many others the trainings have only been routinised exercises, with no real commitment to enhancing people's abilities to engage with such structures.

The introduction of formal institutions in which new rules are prescribed and the expected submission to these leads to the creation of new tensions within communities. Typically, socio-cultural life-worlds, with their own sets of norms and expectations for members of a community, are confronted with the rules and norms of the new institutions through which systemic integration is sought to be realised (Calhoun 1991). Such systemic integration into new institutions requires the fostering of formal relationships and the subscribing to new rules and norms. What results is thereby 'a disconnection of the everyday realm of more and less [sic] successful practical action from the "larger picture" of self-regulating systems, bureaucracies, fragmentation, repression, and the like' (ibid.: 114). This is particularly apposite for us to understand the tensions between communities that seek to retain subscription to their own culture and life-worlds, and also engage with the new structures and processes. In such contexts, they are expected by the state to subscribe to new rules of democracy, and to accept provisioning such as that of elementary education. Resistance from particular groups such as nomads, itinerant groups, and sometimes religious minorities are examples of such tensions between the life-worlds of cultural communities and their integration into the system of the nation-state.

In addition, although most policies that promote 'community-based administration of schools' overlook the class basis[9] of communities, trends indicate that the idea of a community engaging collectively with a school may be challenged by the proliferation of schools within a settlement or a community. For, as both secondary data for schools and ethnographic data from various regions indicate,[10] there is a proliferation of a variety of schools, catering to different cultural and social aspirations of people and their differential economic ability to afford private schooling. Such 'school differentiation'[11] erodes the very structural and cultural abilities of communities to engage with, and contribute to, the growth and development of a common school.

However, policy documents largely overlook these realities and trends, and envisage the role of communities in elementary education primarily through the decentralisation of elementary education administration (DEEA). Subsequently, the 'vocabulary of legitimation' (Li 1996: 509) on which DEEA is promoted rests on the notions of fostering ownership of schools, making teachers accountable to local people, and improving the efficiency of the schooling system. In reality, the key questions around the efficacy and impact of policy hinge on several conditions and factors, each of which also impacts the fulfilment of the objectives of the programme. Several issues related to the links between the state and communities, the problems of legal processes, institution-building, politicisation of society, community/settlement-school relationships, etc., account for a range of problems that act as bottlenecks in the full realisation of community–school linkages.

The State and Decentralisation of Elementary Education[12]

The promulgation and implementation of legislation and structures by the state has been a key factor in the DEEA. States such as Kerala, Karnataka, Himachal Pradesh, Uttaranchal, Haryana, and Sikkim, which have facilitated general decentralisation of administration linked to the 73rd Amendment, have also formulated and implemented DEEA. In these states, people have engaged with, and contributed to, the establishment and integration of community administration in elementary education. In addition, the support by some civil society organisations and NGOs in these states has facilitated the strengthening of DEEA even in the context of increasing school differentiation. The roles played by the Kerala Sasthra Sahithya Parishad, Lok Jumbish in Rajasthan, M. V. Foundation in Secunderabad, Andhra Pradesh, and the Centre for Child and the Law in Karnataka bear testimony to this. The absence of such organisations in most of the other states has buttressed the indifference and even hostility of the state and/or the education department towards DEEA. Despite the potential of decentralised and community-based organisations to support and cater to the functioning and administration of elementary education, there is a range of problems that beset DEEA.

Some states, which have not initiated general decentralisation of administration, have also not facilitated the implementation of DEEA. While Bihar defied, until recently, the implementation of the Panchayati Raj (local self-administration) Acts themselves, the promulgation and implementation of legislation and the required support have been lagging in states such as Odisha, Uttar Pradesh, and Assam. While West Bengal and Madhya Pradesh have also initiated several programmes to enhance community-based administration, the record is mixed. In West Bengal, for decades the decentralised structures had been largely subordinated to the dominant political party, the Communist Party of India (Marxist), and the structures had not led to a realisation of genuine functioning (Acharya 2002). However, while recent trends indicate some improvement in access (Samaddar 2019), more studies are required to assess if the new political dispensation, the Trinamool Congress, has facilitated better people-led governance of government schools. In Madhya Pradesh, several acts and programmes have been put in place, but their inability to function in the absence of mass people's movements, and the failure of the state government to implement the programmes and to devolve genuine powers and allocate funds, has meant that the acts remain largely empty and have become politically and socially contentious issues (Raina 2002).

In most cases, genuine devolution of power to the decentralised bodies is yet to be fully realised. As one reviewer notes, '...devolution in this respect is hardly taking place. A majority of state governments have given only soft powers to the panchayats with regard to primary education like providing land, monitoring attendance of teachers without the authority to take action, etc.' (Tandon 2002: 19). As a result, in many cases, the structures exist without teeth, and state-mandated and directed processes continue to define the everyday life of schools. In such contexts, the key objectives of enabling local accountability and enhancing community management of schools itself remain distant.

In several states, there has been a lack of clarity of rules, powers, and responsibilities, which has subsequently led to confusion and a dilution of the potential of community contribution to schools.

As with the Panchayat Raj Institutions (PRI), the focus has tended to be on construction activities, rather than on disseminating the idea that all community members and the panchayat system carry responsibility for the overall functioning of the school. As studies by Florestal and Cooper (1997) have elaborated, the lack of clarity, specificity, and due process hinders decentralisation measures, and this has been relevant for experiences in many of the states in India.

Along with inadequate dissemination of knowledge, there has been inadequate allocation of financial and decision-making powers to communities, and/or to elected representatives and structures. In most states, the actual devolution of financial powers is yet to be realised and, therefore, the community administration of schools is watered down to the community becoming a watchdog without powers. Even as members and parents in general are expected to contribute to the development of schools (through the contribution of land and labour) and undertake administrative duties such as monitoring teachers' attendance and ensuring children's attendance in schools, they are largely without the authority to take action if school rules are violated by teachers.

Periodic alterations to the PRI Acts and/or their links to the community administration of schools have also made the structures unstable and dysfunctional. An example is the state of Karnataka, where the establishment of the School Development and Monitoring Committee (SDMC), meant to overcome the limitation of the VEC, has been subject to periodic alteration. Drawing on the pioneering support and institutionalisation of the 73rd Amendment, the state had promulgated and activated a range of community-based organisations such as VECs and School Betterment Committees (SBCs) for DEEA. However, based on the recommendations of the Task Force for Education (2000), the state promulgated the establishment of the SDMCs to address the drawbacks of earlier structures. The SDMCs were to be constituted only by the parents of children from the schools themselves. Associated with this structure was a range of responsibilities, including financial powers to develop infrastructure and authority to oversee the functioning of schools.

Even as this structure was established and reports indicated its largely successful contribution, Members of the Legislative Assembly (MLAs) of the state challenged the structure. The government then issued a notification indicating that the MLAs had the power to nominate the nine members of the SDMCs and the president, and to also become the presidents of the high school SDMCs. This created a furore over the bypassing of grassroots democracy and its usurpation by higher elected representatives, and education activists challenged this in court. A suicide note by a woman teacher in April 2007, alleging continued and unbearable harassment by an SDMC president, led the teachers' union to call for the withdrawal of the SDMCs and for the curtailment of their powers. The Government of Karnataka subsequently instituted a committee to review this, and the judgment by the High Court that followed facilitated the reinstatement of SDMCs, as linked to the PRIs or decentralised administration system. New SDMCs were then elected along the lines of the new by-laws, which link SDMCs to the PRIs, and also stipulate that only parents of the school attendees are to be members of the SDMC (Niranjanaradhya n.d.).

The increasing politicisation of society, and the spread and presence of political parties in the lives of citizens have also led to the politicisation of many institutions. Political parties have sought to capture these institutions, both as sites in which their powers can be extended and as ways to allocate powers to their members and to garner support. As a result, schools and their management structures have become important sites of such political contestations (Noronha 2003; Vasavi 2006b). Reports from across the country testify to this,[13] and the extreme cases, such as in West Bengal and Kerala, where these structures had been captured and integrated into the political apparatus of dominant political parties, have also been documented.

These problems of administration then manifest or lead to other problems in the elementary education system. As studies (PROBE 1999) of the problems of quality in elementary education have indicated, the absence of adequate administration and management, and failure to ensure the accountability of teachers remain at the root of most problems of inadequate teaching-learning hours and non-utilisation of training.

SOME SOCIO-POLITICAL QUERIES ON COMMUNITIES IN EDUCATION

The above details about the possibilities and problems of forging community-school relations, after an interim of nearly 140 years, pose several socio-political questions. For one, given the context of introducing an idea, or more specifically, the reintroduction of a relationship that was disrupted, what has been the significance of the constitution of the institutions (for both the school and the decentralised structure) and the outcomes expected from it? Unlike the pre-colonial context, when schools had identities as local institutions, the contemporary identity of schools as predominantly government institutions makes for a significant difference. The state, through its mass schooling, marks the content, orientation, schedule, and impact of education, making it primarily a de-localised institution, subject to bureaucratic structures, processes, and stipulated outcomes. Hence, blueprints that seek to forge or establish community–school relations focus only on structures of administration that can facilitate localised, parental inputs to improve the functioning of schools and the accountability of teachers. Given this structure and orientation, the new community–school linkages are fraught with many contradictions. Even as parents and local community members are expected to bear the burden and responsibility of the school's functioning, they have little or no role in the content of school knowledge, practices, and its orientation. Recent trends that indicate a drive towards an enhanced role for the global restructuring of education, with its potential to further distance communities from education, only highlight the irony of such administrative techniques.

However, inasmuch as such restructuring is also located within attempts and policies to deepen democracy, the viability and significance of such decentralisation must also be factored in. In fact, Mahmood Mamdani's (2001) observation for South Africa, that the departments for 'local government' are really departments for the control and capture of peasants, is largely true for India as well. Governmental reach into the realms of village, community, and family has been deployed through various agencies, such as the departments of agriculture, agricultural extension, community development, health, and elementary education. While such reach has led to the over-politicisation of social life in rural India (Tanabe 2007) and to the multiple contestations over development and politics (Sivaramakrishnan 2000), the significance of these various programmes for the very identity and reproduction of 'communities' is yet to be studied.

In the larger context of the spread of advanced technology, post-industrialisation, globalisation, and mediatisation, the 'coming community' (Agamben 2007) is postulated to be closer to a simulacra[14] of spectacles generated by the media and the market, which relate to the public as consumers. But for disadvantaged societies lying on the periphery of globalisation and post-industrialisation, which are subject to processes of disembedding of their economic, social, and political life, the idea of the 'global village' is indeed a cruel irony. Even as they stand to lose some positive features of being viable communities, many will experience significant alterations, which may not be similar to the simulacra communities. As such communities undergo changes, either through their earlier fuzzy boundaries being reconstituted within rigid boundaries defined by caste, religious, regional, or ethnic identities, or in their engagement with forms of modernity and democracy, their links with formal structures and institutions are also bound to change. Compounding this are the variations in the economic-political configurations of community members, which will also redefine their alliances with agencies of the state and the market. Perhaps the emergence of communities as political actors, with local and translocal identities and ambitions, will soon be one of the key defining principles in community–school interlinkages. But the irony of a situation in which ideas and policies based on fostering 'community participation' are promoted, even as organic communities themselves are in states of disarray and displacement, needs to be reckoned with.

Definitions and expectations of 'communities' to be organic wholes that can undertake administrative responsibilities, without adequate and continued support from the state, overlook the increasing disembeddedness[15] and deterritorialisation to which they are subject, and in some cases, the new identities which they are crafting for themselves. While factoring all these in, there must be recognition that community participation cannot conjure up images of complete contribution and engagement of all communities with respect to issues of elementary education, or of communities as having the potential to bear all the responsibilities. Instead, 'the kind of participation that is likely to be the most sustainable and effective in increasing both educational access and quality is one based on balanced partnerships between the state and communities...' (Swift-Morgan 2006: 365).

But the key challenge of realising the most important potential of community–school linkages remains—that is, the assertion of rights by communities to engage with the education of their children, by eventually administering their own elementary education system. In this context, can the African saying, 'It takes a village to bring up a child' be relevant in India? While our contemporary complex and contested predicament indicates this to be fraught with challenges, it should be with this hope that programmes for community–school linkages must be sustained.

NOTES

Acknowledgements: This is a revised version of an unpublished paper I had presented at the seminar organised in 2009 at NUEPA, New Delhi on 'Communities and Schools'. I would like to thank Dr Avinash Singh for initiating this engagement. Some of the details for the paper are drawn from the elementary education project, Vidyankura, supported by the NIAS, Bangalore, and the Sir Ratan Tata Trust, Mumbai, and based in Chamarajanagar district, Karnataka.

1. The historical existence and functioning of viable village-level bodies for local administration have been recorded in India, but their democratic and representative characteristics in the pre-Independence period are open to debate. In several British colonial provinces, as

also in parts of princely India, efforts were directed at promoting decentralised administration, but the experiments were patchy and subject to periodic revision through differing laws (see Daswani et al. 1997 for a brief note on this).

2. The following documents pertaining to community-school relations were reviewed: GoI (1996, 1998), UNESCO (1997), and a range of short reports pertaining to DPEP and Sarva Shiksha Abhiyan programmes in the various states.
3. See NIAS (2002a, 2002b) for ethnographic details on the problem of locating 'community-based' initiatives in urban poverty areas.
4. B. R. Ambedkar was sharply critical of Gandhi's idealisation of Indian villages, and called them a den of vice and a cesspool of caste politics.
5. I refer to the term 'social capital' as explicated by Robert Putnam (1993), that is, as a characteristic in which members of a group/s have mutual trust between them and are capable of acting as a corporate group. Although I do not endorse this as a valid factor that determines advantage or abilities of groups and communities, I draw on this since many policy documents endorse this idea in a vicarious and implicit way.
6. Since most of the policy and programme documents focus on rural settlements and communities, I have also concentrated on delineating trends in rural settlement communities with some mention of trends in urban communities, especially those in poverty areas.
7. Some of the recent studies that delineate the post-liberalisation trends in India are those by Sanyal (2007), John et al. (2006), and a range of articles in the *Economic and Political Weekly.*
8. Tanabe (2007) contextualises his description of a 'post, post-colonial' society by drawing on the definitions of civil society as that which mediates between the family and the state, political society (as defined by Partha Chatterjee), as associations formed by the poor and disenfranchised (as population) who seek to garner or demand benefits from the state, and a moral society which Tanabe defines as one in which people draw on practical-moral relationships to negotiate in the wider socio-political world.
9. See Herring and Agarwala (2006) for a discussion on the neglect of class issues and perspectives in India, and the implications of this for the study of India.
10. Data on number of schools in the nation indicates a gradual but sure increase in the number of non-government schools. In 2004–2005,

89 per cent of primary schools were government-run, 2.5 per cent were aided but privately managed, and only 7.24 per cent were fully privately owned. Ethnographic studies such as those by NIAS (2002) and the study by Geeta Gandhi Kingdon (2007) indicate the growth in low-fee private schools, especially in urban areas.

11. The idea of 'school differentiation' has been elaborated in an earlier publication (see Vasavi 2019a), and is a chapter in this volume (see Chapter 3).
12. Details for the following section are largely drawn from an earlier report, 'Management Structures: Mid Project Review of EFA in India', developed for the MHRD and NUEPA by Rahul Mukhopadhyay et al. (2007).
13. For studies from various states on problems of devolution of panchayat powers, especially pertaining to elementary education administration, see Acharya (2002), Niranjanaradhya (n.d.), Noronha (2003), Sharan (2007), and Tandon (2002).
14. 'Simulacra' refers to the processes of imitation or replication of a dominant model or prototype. Such communities lose their distinctive identities and features and are absorbed into the larger political-economies as subordinate entities.
15. Disembeddedness refers to processes of change where foundational features of any society or community are altered and cease to have significance for the local community or society.

V

'GOVERNMENT BRAHMIN'

Caste, the Educated Unemployed, and the Reproduction of Inequalities

It is now twelve years since I started to take competitive exams. I have cleared some written exams, but did not make it through the interviews. In 2010, I cleared the exam and interview for the High School Headmaster's post. But I am still waiting to get my allocated post. If I can get this job, then I will be secure and able to fend for myself and my family, including my mother, and sister's family. I don't know if I can pursue my interests in art, but right now a secure job and regular income are important.

Selections from the diary of B. Mallesha,[1] 2012,
as translated from Kannada by the author.

In Mallesha's travails concerning the securing of a government job lies the complex trajectory of a person from a 'Scheduled Caste'[2] seeking education, employment, and security. Mallesha's life represents the limitations of formal and institutionalised structures of educational opportunity for disadvantaged groups in India. Even as debates and public pressure both in favour of and against affirmative action in education and employment continue, the labelling of affirmative action candidates as 'Government Brahmins'[3] highlights the attendant hostility and resentment that such programmes invoke. Seen and labelled as undeserving candidates, who have now become the new elite through government largesse, there is often an absence of attention to the multiple disadvantages that such candidates experience.

The details of Mallesha's engagement and experience with various institutions, established to create 'equality of opportunity' and to facilitate the development and capability of citizens, indicate multiple complexities. The disadvantages of a sub-standard education, heavy family responsibilities, lack of social and cultural capital, and intensification of corruption in the very institutions that should enable equality of opportunity become hurdles in Mallesha's attempts at improving his life. What he stands to sacrifice are his own interests and skills, which governmental endeavours such as reservation/positive discrimination—forms of creating equality of opportunity—overlook in their emphasis on integrating persons into the mainstream, albeit sub-standard, models of development and equality. Perhaps what stands out the most in Mallesha's case—which is representative of the situation and predicament of a large number of youth, including SC/ST youth (up to sixty-five lakhs[4]), who are seeking legitimacy, recognition, and integration into a dominant system—is his attempt to access and gain entry into the large government apparatus, which is seen as a key source of not only economic and social mobility, but also of social recognition. The emphasis and spread of such a hegemonic model contain and reproduce several inequities and disadvantages.

The dominant economic model is built on the negation of plural and diverse practices and forms of livelihoods and life-worlds. In privileging a model in which both development and equality are premised on ideas of fostering the transition of a large mass of people from an agrarian or non-industrial/non-urban economy to a predominantly urban/industrial economy via opportunities for education, little attention is paid to the crafting of alternatives in which multiple skills, abilities, and life-worlds can be created or sustained. At the same time, the emphasis on mainstreaming persons into the dominant education and employment model overlooks how long-entrenched structures of 'graded inequality'[5] (Ambedkar 1945 [1936]) work at micro and macro levels to reproduce forms of inequality. Such inequality includes the continued hold of caste-based disadvantages at a formative stage of people's lives, as also the persistence of caste-based discrimination, corruption, and violation of rights, even at the levels of formal institutions such as schools, universities, and recruitment agencies.

Both visible and invisible barriers exist that reproduce conditions of exclusion and deprivation. Even as the rhetoric of 'inclusive growth' and 'inclusive policies' gains currency, it is important to assess how the very agendas of inclusion strengthen pre-existing and entrenched forms of inequalities. India's post-1991 economy has meant that the marginalised, who are also the majority, are located primarily as a depleted class, while what has become dominant is an enticing, glittering economy, which is after all an illusory enclave economy led by global financial capital. For the marginalised people, who are located primarily outside this spectral and speculative economy, it is their disembedded and continuously eroded lives and livelihoods that are the key markers of their personhood and being. Such trends indicate the need to recognise the voice and agency of disadvantaged groups and persons, especially in the context of understanding their experiences of public institutions and the impact that these institutions have on them. Weis and Fine's (2012: 174) notion of critical bifocality, which seeks to 'make visible the sinewy linkages or circuits through which structural conditions are enacted in policy and reform institutions as well as the ways in which such conditions come to be woven into community relationships and metabolised by individuals', is useful, and enables one to make interlinkages between the macro policies that claim to promote equality of opportunity and the experiences of those whom such policies seek to serve.

Contextualising Mallesha's experiences at several levels and tracing the interlinkages to macro structures, processes, and institutions enable persons like him to represent themselves through new forms of ethnography[6] that can encapsulate both subjective experiences and objective structuring factors. Drawing on details from his diary and supplementing these with discussions with him and observations on trends related to his experience enable one to assess the realisation of official pronouncements and the impact of these policies on the life-worlds of people.

Standard and official narratives disseminated by official bodies concerned with economic development and growth identify a range of factors and conditions that produce and reproduce inequalities.

The World Bank, as the dominant apparatus that claims to address forms of inequalities, sees inequality as 'objectionable on both intrinsic and instrumental grounds. It contributes to economic inefficiency, political conflict, and institutional frailty' (World Bank 2006: 9). Overlooking how inequality erodes the very sense of being of so many marginal and disadvantaged persons, the World Bank sees the creation of 'equality of opportunities' as one of the key ways of addressing national-level inequalities. The opportunities are identified as access to education, health, resources, and infrastructure, all of which, in the myriad policy documents and discourses, are sought to be translated into objectives and measurable criteria. Perhaps what has been missed in all these is the persistence and reproduction of 'existential inequality', which Göran Therborn[7] (2009) identifies as inequalities which affect and mark individuals, whereby there is a denial of recognition and respect. It is the form and entrenchment of this inequality that accounts for what is seen as a contradiction—the inability of the people, inspite of their strength in numbers, to challenge the very sources, structures, and agencies of debilitating inequalities.

Mallesha's life is marked by inequalities, the sources of which lie in the life-conditions of family and community, schooling and education, and employment structures and strictures. Locating the life narratives of such persons and their attempts to negotiate the multiple disadvantages through the dominant system and its prescriptions will highlight the complex issues involved in addressing inequality through the mechanisms of education, employment, and integration into the dominant apparatus.

Mallesha's Origins

Mallesha has an MA in History and a B.Ed. degree. He is also an artist and signboard painter, and resides in Kollegal town, Karnataka, India. At the age of thirty-two, Mallesha's life has been marked by many inequities, including the 'poverty trap' that prevents him, his family, and also members of his neighbourhood-cum-caste community from moving out of conditions of marginality and multiple forms of inequality.

Family and Community

> I was born into a Scheduled Caste family and belong to the Madiga (leather workers) sub-caste.[8] My parents were uneducated. I am the eldest son and I have a younger brother and sister. When I was studying in Standard I, my father passed away. We had only one small shack as our own property. We had no other property or money. My mother and all of us (three) children moved into my paternal grandparents' house, and we lived there for four years along with our paternal uncle. After that, because of the frequent quarrels in the family, we were separated from the larger family and started to live independently. My mother, who had no knowledge at all of the larger world, started making a living by working at construction sites, spinning silk reels at home, cooking food for sale, grinding rice and millets for others, etc. Somehow, she managed to bring us up. Observing all these problems, our maternal uncles sent our youngest uncle to look after us. He worked as a head loader [one who loads/transports construction material like bricks, cement etc. by carrying on their heads] in the Kollegal bus stand and, together with my mother, looked after us.

Research has increasingly highlighted that class background, parental occupations, and living conditions influence both educational performance and aspirations (Booth and Crouter 2001; Lareau 2003). Yet research in India has failed to detail how intra-family locations and caste-community relations vis-à-vis the larger society and politico-economic factors act as deterrents to those aspiring and working towards educational achievements. Although there has recently been recognition of intra-family inequalities which go beyond the macro and structural sources of inequality, adequate attention has not been paid to the multiple burdens that individuals bear within these families, and to the demands that families impose on children. For example, the *World Development Report 2006*, with its focus on 'Equity and Development', highlights how '... income and expenditure are often controlled by the male members of the family and that this leads to underinvestment, especially in the health and education of girls' (World Bank 2006: 104). The focus on intra-family issues, then, has been primarily on gender-related differences, with some attention being paid to how patriarchy and male dominance reproduce varied forms of inequality. What is missing in these narratives is the reproduction of inequalities that are embedded in the family- and community-based structures. Subsequently, the very strategies of survival that these disadvantaged families deploy to overcome inequality and poverty are reproduced over generations.

While Mallesha and his siblings were fortunate to have a larger extended family that sustained them in the early years, he, like many of the oldest children in working-class families, internalised the idea of acting as the *de facto* head of the family. The premature death of the earning parent becomes the single biggest burden on children, and is often the key factor in children dropping out of school and joining the pool of child workers. Children of single parents, in most cases those without fathers, often take on adult roles at a young age and act as parents to their younger siblings (NIAS 2002a).

> I started supporting my family when I was in Standard X (at about fifteen years of age). I worked as an apprentice to a painter and he would pay me some money. That way, I contributed to the household. When I was studying for my Bachelor's degree, I went to work in the afternoons and evenings since my classes were only in the mornings. I was able to support my brother's studies also. Even though I dropped out of CAVA, Mysore (a fine arts college), I insisted that my brother finish the five-year course there, and later, I also got him enrolled into the Master of Fine Arts course in Bangalore. My sister was not keen on studies and dropped out of high school. Since my sister and her husband [who is also Mallesha's maternal uncle; the family practices maternal uncle-niece marriage which is common among several communities in South India] live with us, I continue to look after them. Uncle looked after us when we were young and dependent. So, now I look after his extra expenses. I paid for my sister's delivery charges, including hospitalisation and care for the premature baby. Once I was able to get more regular work, I stopped my mother from working outside the house, and she only looked after the house. My family consults me on all matters and listens to me. I also take care of all their needs.

Neighbourhood

> My neighbourhood [a settlement of about 180–200 households, just off the Kollegal-Bangalore highway] has mostly Madiga (leather workers) households. When we were young, most of the men were occupied in leather-related work. My father purchased sheep and goats which were then sold for meat. Nowadays, many of the men work as head loaders, construction workers, drivers, and painters, and some go to the cotton and sugarcane mills. Most of the women stay at home and do household work. Only in those families that have no earning male member do the women go out to work in the mills or to the grain centres to clean grains.
>
> There used to be a lot of alcoholism when I was growing up. There were frequent and violent fights in the families. Many children dropped out of school as their fathers were drunkards and either did not support the families, or died when they were young. Nowadays, drinking has decreased. Some of those who suffered from this are now conscious and want to give their children a better life.
>
> Most of the youth in the neighbourhood are able to study only up to high school. Only some go on to pre-university [that is, pre-Bachelor degree courses] but many drop out from here also. There were about six to eight of us, all boys, who went to college. Nowadays, girls go for D. Ed. (Diploma in Education). There is pressure on girls to get jobs to help with dowry payments. Girls with jobs also find it easier to get husbands.

Education and 'Capability Development'

With the post-Jomtien Conference's[9] emphasis on education as the key driver of capability development, the dominant development discourse claims that basic education is the foundation on which development is made possible, and promotes it. Echoing such perspectives, popular sentiment among the SC groups sees caste-based educational deprivation that denied them the right to formal learning (and literacy) as the single biggest factor that has hindered their exit out of poverty, discrimination, and low status. Education, as formal learning, is sought as a way out of a life of hardship and as a route to a better life. Families repose great faith in the ability of education to enable them to address their multiple disadvantages, and many people even go hungry in order to get their children educated. For Mallesha, school as an opportunity was a mixed experience.

School

> I studied in a school run by Catholic priests and we did not pay any fees. I went to this school regularly until Standard IV, and they used to teach us very well. I was also a good student. The teachers were very strict and we had 'bhaya-bhakti' (fear and devotion) about them. One day, in Standard IV, a teacher caned me on my hand. Out of fear of this punishment, I did not go to school for a year. Because I did not attend school, they also beat me at home. My mother would give me a good beating and then cry. Once, they heated an iron rod and burnt me on my back. But still, I was very stubborn and did not go to school. Even when my classmates came to call me, I would not go. One day, some students from Standard VII came to my house and carried me to school. Still, I did not attend school. So, after all these attempts, they sent me to graze goats. After a year, my grandfather took me again to the school and re-admitted me. All the teachers spoke to me gently. They advised me to come to school regularly. At this time, I was studying with students who were younger than me, but still I did well in class. In Standard V, I was selected to go for a drawing competition. I did not know how to draw well. The other students, who had come from different schools, knew how to draw. They all had sketch pens, colour pencils, paints and paint brushes, etc. I had not seen any of these. Seeing all this, I had a desire that I too must learn how to draw and get all these things. From that day, I started to practice drawing. With this, I was able to distinguish myself from the others. I continued to learn and practice drawing even during my studies for various degrees. Some of the teachers supported me in this.

The trauma of entering formal educational institutions which are hostile and not particularly child-friendly is rarely documented. For many children from marginalised families, among whom formal and regimented learning is non-existent, such experiences become the bases for dropping out. Mallesha's case is exceptional in that his grandfather was insistent that he attend school, and he was fortunate to have sensitive teachers who recognised his interests and abilities and encouraged him.

Illness

> When I was in Standard VI, I developed a severe allergy to dust. I would get fits of cough and cold and had to stay away from school. I had to be taken to the hospital frequently. My mother also took several vows dedicated to various gods and goddesses. She took me to several temples, mathas,[10] and religious fairs. I had several amulets around my neck, on my arm, and around my waist. Through all this, I would vent my anger on my mother and throw all the amulets away. Mother sold her brass vessels, her earrings, and also borrowed heavily to treat my ailment. It was only when I started going to pre-university college that the allergies subsided.

Ill health, resulting primarily from malnutrition, marks the lives of many children from marginalised families. While health services and institutions are difficult to access, popular understanding of illness also emphasises treatment through the appeasement of spirits, demons, and deities. Mallesha's early experiences traumatised him sufficiently to make him sceptical of such health-seeking practices. Yet, his early childhood conditions made him vulnerable to frequent bouts of ill health, which would be a setback later in his life.

Educational Institutions: Social Scarring and Humiliation

The expansion of the education system into a form of mass and public development agenda has meant that issues of education quality (in terms of learning levels and the functioning of the institutions) have become matters of serious concern. The very orientation and functioning of these institutions mean that they, in most cases, do not facilitate a comprehensive endowment (that stands for a range of social and cultural capital along with market-recognised skills and knowledge/certification) or capability of different persons. Recent reviews and reports have consistently indicated the extant poor quality of education in government primary schools (ASER 2014), which are now largely attended by children of the low-ranked caste groups. Similarly, there are also studies that critique the lack of quality in the provisioning of relevant or employment-oriented education even at the secondary and higher education levels. But there are very few studies that detail the alienating environment and the severe limitations of the new mass educational institutions. Policy discourse that focuses on promoting increased access to higher education completely overlooks these considerations and issues.

The development discourse also places much faith in the ability of institutions to endow and entitle individuals and disadvantaged groups with a range of new capabilities. Institutions of education, especially, are seen and represented as carriers of development and as enabling the addressing of inequalities. Where there is recognition of the very problematic nature of institutions, it is qualified and identified as emanating primarily from either political or economic institutions. For example, although the World Bank report recognises how '... complex historical processes, combined with inequalities in influence and power, may lead to bad political and economic institutions which severely impair the development of poor countries' (2006: 8), there is little recognition of the social scarring of marginalised individuals and groups in and by educational institutions.

Although Mallesha and his friends, as members of the socially low-ranked and officially 'Scheduled Caste' groups, are admitted to the university and its hostels on the basis of 'affirmative action' or educational 'reservations', their experience of the educational institution and its endowment does not further their capability development, or their knowledge and skills to compete in the employment market. The lack of attention to providing quality education and the general limitations[11] of India's affirmative education policy (Weisskopf 2004) are manifest in Mallesha's experience of university life. More specifically, the expansion of, and even the emphasis on, equity through affirmative education policies have not addressed the 'institutional handicaps and handicaps in life-history' (Bögenhold 2001: 833), which continue to mark the lives of even educated persons from disadvantaged backgrounds.[12]

> Since I was interested in art and many of the teachers recognised this, I thought I should join CAVA (Chamarajendra Academy of Visual Arts), a fine arts training centre in Mysore. I had saved about Rs 6,000 and gained entry to CAVA after passing the tests. I had also spoken with my paternal uncles and they promised to help pay the fees for the two-year course. However, I was able to attend only for three months. The materials (paints, brushes, sketch books, etc.) were very expensive. As a Scheduled Caste student, I received a stipend of only Rs 150 per month. This was not adequate. When I approached my uncles for financial help, they dithered. So, I dropped out of CAVA.
>
> I later joined the Bachelor of Arts (BA) course in Kollegal itself. The classes were only in the morning, and I worked in the evenings. Since I stayed at home, there were no extra expenses for hostel or food. But, even after completing my BA course here, I was not able to get a job. I then decided to enrol for a Master's course in History. I enrolled in Mysore University. The teachers were indifferent. They rarely took classes. We had a few textbooks and only some of us went to the library. There were no good discussions or interaction between the teachers and the students. We, as students from small towns and villages, were always hesitant. They (the teachers) talked down to us.
>
> Every month, there were at least two strikes, and classes were cancelled. On the non-strike days, classes were conducted only until the afternoon and after that most students whiled away time in the hostels. The facilities were also not good in the hostel. I used to try and be preoccupied with drawing or writing banners, but I did not get such work continuously. The students had groups, and caste associations were strong. Friendships and alliances were made on the bases of their links with their villages and/or their caste groups. I did not join any of them.
>
> Our hostel life in Mysore was very difficult. I stayed at the 'Backward Classes Hostel' run by the Department of Social Welfare. Every student who had gained entry into the hostel legally had to support at least two or three friends who had entered through the 'back door'. They ate at the mess (dining facilities) and also lived in the rooms. The running of the mess was auctioned to outsiders, and they always

> sought to make money and gave us food that was inadequate and of poor quality. There were often fights over this. The authorities accused students of misusing the mess and bringing in friends. The students accused the authorities of being corrupt and of 'swallowing' the money allocated by the government for them. The hostel also did not have any library facilities. Since classes were held only until the afternoon, we whiled away the time after that. We could not afford to buy our own books. No one cared for us, and the students, in turn, became indifferent to rules and to their own lives. I think we wasted our time there. There was little learning and many students picked up bad habits (drinking, gambling, and wasting time).
>
> Exams were held only once a year. But our performance in these was not always even. Only a few among us did well. Many would fail or get low marks. There were always fights over this, just as there were fights over the food and the hostel. General caste students often referred to us as 'Government Brahmins' (Government Brahmanaru). We know that even some teachers did so. They considered us unworthy of the reservations and believed we were there only because the government was supporting us. There was always tension about this.

'Government Brahmins'

The general tension in the campus is compounded by the limitations of most educational programmes. These include the failure to engage students adequately or to provide updated syllabi and content, and the submission to populist demands, because of which the overall content and quality are further eroded.

The reservation policy and the programme designed to address inherited disadvantages fail to develop abilities and skills among these aspiring youth. Hostilities and rivalries between caste groups lead to the labelling of SC students, and those others who receive reservations in institutions, as 'Government Brahmins'—those privileged by the largesse of the government. Intense competition over limited educational seats, deep-rooted prejudices among upper-caste students and faculty, and the institutional failure to facilitate inter-caste integration have led to some of these hostilities. Popular perception, which deems the access of low-ranked caste groups to education as undeserving and wasteful, fails to assess the deep problems in the provisioning of such education, which is largely inadequate, poor in quality, and which also fails to enable many to break out of their conditions of disadvantage.

Such tensions in the politics of redistribution and recognition were noted by Nancy Fraser (1997: 25):

> 'Affirmative Redistribution' ... aims to redress economic injustice, (but) it leaves intact the deep structures that generate class disadvantage. Thus, it must make surface relocations again and again. The result is to mark the most disadvantaged class as inherently deficient and insatiable, as always needing more and more. In time, such a class even more comes to appear privileged, the recipient of special treatment and undeserved largesse. Thus, an approach aimed at redressing injustices of distribution can end up creating injustices of recognition.

This is precisely what has become the norm in most educational campuses in India, accompanied by the rhetoric that 'undeserving', 'non-merit', and 'poorly qualified' students from low-ranked caste groups have now gained entry and are largely responsible for the decline in the standard of education. This is compounded by hostilities between student groups, which are drawn largely on caste lines. In what is a cruel misnomer, reserved category students began to be referred to as 'Government Brahmins', which mocks them as unqualified for their reserved seat privilege. High dropout rates among the reserved category students, and growing hostilities and anxieties in various institutions over academic performance and the treatment of such students have become rampant across the nation.

Dreams of English

Submitting to regional language politics, which by the 1980s had gained momentum in Karnataka, many universities diluted their standards of higher education, by not lecturing in English, permitting students to write examination papers for all subjects in Kannada, and allowing even the submission of all dissertations in Kannada. The first casualty of this was the large mass of first-generation college students, primarily from rural and low-ranked caste groups, who were permitted to receive education in the state language, Kannada. While the number of graduates increased, their worth in the job market decreased dramatically. Ruing the lack of English-language teaching and the fact that he, and his friends and classmates, are unable to even speak in English; Mallesha expresses deep regret and discomfort.

> In school, we were taught English from Standard V onwards. The teachers themselves did not know English. They memorised a few words and sentences and pretended to read. They let us write the words in Kannada over the English words so that we could read them. We mostly memorised the passages and could barely understand anything. We could not speak it, even though nowadays some of us can read ... the newspapers. It was the same in college. They allowed us to read, write, and take the exams in Kannada. We found this easy and did not have to struggle. But, we know that knowing English helps get jobs. Many of those who have failed in Standard X did so because they failed in English. Even in college, we were not encouraged to know English. Now, we try. But we can only dream about English.

UNEMPLOYABILITY

Policy documents and reports which focus on criteria such as increasing the number or proportion of graduates, etc., are singled out as key to the assessment of development. However, lack of attention to the quality of education, and the sacrifice of quality at the altar of assertions of quantity means that the disadvantaged become doubly disadvantaged. Lack of knowledge of English prevents them from being employed in the urban and new service sectors. In the contradictory and complex turn of an increasingly globalising economy, Mallesha and his friends read about new job opportunities in the nation's metropolises, for example, a booming IT and IT-enabled services (ITeS) economy has taken off in the regional capital, Bengaluru, where jobs are aplenty for those who can speak English. But many of these unemployed youth, mostly those with poor quality education and lacking skills for the new economy, are described as 'unemployable', often assigning individual blame for such limitations. Even mainstream discourse overlooks the institutional and structural limitations due to which these disadvantaged youth are rendered 'unemployable'. These youths desperately forge multiple strategies to gain entry into mainstream or government jobs. Distanced from any possibility of gaining entry into the new global economy and unwilling to do agricultural work and/or engage in manual labour or their caste-based work, as these are considered demeaning and insulting for educated persons, many youths wander across different educational institutions, courses, and short-term assignments that provide them little or no skills for employment. Caste-based skills such as smithy, carpentry, tanning and leather work, stonework, weaving, etc., are neglected or forgotten as none of these skills are recognised in even the vocational training courses offered by the Industrial Training Institutes (ITI). The expansion of the higher education system, primarily through a network of colleges and regional/state universities, has been at the cost of providing quality and relevant education. Most institutions, outdated in content, orientation, and modes of training, produce graduates who remain unemployed, underemployed, or unemployable in the new economy. The lack of competence in English is only one of the key handicaps faced by those who receive this mass higher education. For many, formal education does not provide them with the capability to compete in the job market, or with sufficient skill to become independent entrepreneurs or workers.

The Spectre and Treadmill of Competitive Examinations

Over the years, Mallesha acquired several degrees. Apart from completing the two-year pre-degree course in Arts (History, Kannada, and Geography), he worked to get a Bachelor's degree (BA in History), a Master's degree (MA in History), and a B.Ed. (Bachelor's degree in Education). Like many of his compatriots in his neighbourhood, he appeared for several competitive examinations in order to get a government job. Each attempt, a prolonged process often taking several years (between applying for the post and receiving the final decision), marks every aspirant as having either 'passed' or 'failed'.

> For most of us in the neighbourhood, a job in the government is seen as the best opportunity. Government jobs (government *kelasa*) are considered to provide security (*badrathe*), are permanent (*khayam*), and also have prestige (*gaurava*). Even a low-level government employee has high status and is regarded with respect. Most of the boys start to take exams for government jobs as soon as they pass Standard X. Many take the exams for first-division and second-division clerks. Others also take the many exams for teachers' posts, for the forest department, and the revenue and the police departments.
>
> Over the past ten years, I have taken several exams. I have appeared for the High School Teachers' exams thrice, and once each for the posts of pre-university college lecturer, revenue inspector, hostel warden, and first division clerk. I have taken the Karnataka Education Service Exam once and the Karnataka Administrative Service exam twice.[13]

A Funnel System: Entry Barriers and Corruption

Mallesha provides details of the dates for the examinations on which he had pinned his hopes. The process for competing for the high school headmasters' post is as follows:

1. Submission of application: December 2007
2. Preliminary examination (objective type): February 2008
3. Results of Preliminary: June 2008
4. Main (descriptive) examination: December 2008
5. Results of Main examination: July 2009; call for interview
6. Interview: September 2009
7. Final list of selected candidates: February 2010
8. Appointment letter: Sent in June 2012

The process, stretching over four years, involves the assessment of a large number of applicants. For the final 629 posts which were available, at least 60,000–80,000 applicants took the examinations.

Of these, only about a 1,000 were able to clear them, and qualified for the interview. Even as the whole process is delayed and no details or dates are shared with the candidates, the issue of the number of posts available remains contested.

Over the years, the increasing demand for such government jobs and the gradual shrinking of these posts has meant that the very institutions that process such examinations and job allocations have also become very corrupt. Even as formal and mechanised processes (objective-type questions assessed by computers) of examination are introduced, the final selection (interviews) becomes the key stage in which influence and money power work to get candidates the job. Applicants seek the help of caste-based politicians or organisations to either support their candidacy or help them negotiate the system in terms of bribing selection officers directly or indirectly. In Karnataka, the state's Public Service Commission became the object of much public ridicule and speculation.[14] Standing out as an institution with the responsibility of recruiting and allocating government jobs, the state's Public Service Commission has become the antithesis of its very mandate. Far from being open and public- or service-oriented, it has become an institution run by successive governments as an agency for realising party- or caste-affiliated ambitions, and expanding the pool of government employees who will owe allegiance and support to them. Malpractice and irregularities in recruitment led the former chairman, responsible for recruitment over a period of years, to be investigated; he was subsequently served a notice and imprisoned.[15] Between 2010 and 2011, the selection of external headmasters, the post for which Mallesha applied, became contested. Even as 629 posts were declared, older teachers, who were also eligible for the post of headmaster as part of their career advancement, filed a petition in court challenging the education department's recruitment of outsiders. As the court case dragged on, some of the aspirants who had cleared the examinations went on a hunger strike. A compromise was sought, which was to be hammered out between the Teachers' Association that opposed the new recruitment and the new recruits who were still awaiting appointment.[16] Such delays, confusion, and lack of transparency make the whole process of state-based recruitment for employment even more fraught with tension.

'Competitive exams' or examinations for professional educational courses or for government jobs have become a spectre in the lives of the marginal youth. They immerse themselves in applying for, preparing for, and taking several competitive exams, and then waiting for the results with their aspirations centred on being successful in any one of them. Even as they witness the booming urban economy, their own opportunities have not only shrunk, but are also marked by processes that deny them their individuality, creativity, and interest. In the increasingly competitive and corrupt context of gaining government jobs, the youth experience multiple forms of humiliation and degradation. Much of the discussion and preparation for the exams revolve around guessing and discerning what the contents of the exam will be, and anticipating who will be on the interview board. Preparations for written exams involve purchasing 'guidebooks', especially those which focus on preparing candidates for a range of exams. Gathering in friends' homes or in public places, groups of friends attempt 'model exam papers' and discuss ways in which the exam can be 'cracked'. In all of this, an in-depth knowledge of issues and subject matter is completely bypassed. For those taking multiple exams, the target is to gain competence in the different types of exams (objective type or written essays), and they seek extra help in order to succeed.

Mallesha himself became one such 'government job seeker'—an appellation that has gained currency and even legitimacy among the youth as they await jobs. A relaxation in the age bar for SC candidates means that he is eligible to take these exams until the age of thirty-five. This extended age entitlement is also the basis on which Mallesha and his friends pin their hopes of gaining entry into the government sector. It also means they neglect other avenues and fail to seek opportunities elsewhere. For the disadvantaged youth, whose singular objective in adult life is to obtain a 'government job', the delays, the lack of transparency, and the entry of questionable and inadequately trained persons into the system compel them to view the whole edifice and process of recruitment for government jobs as a corrupt enterprise. Scams that break out indicate not only nepotism, but also the purchase of jobs through bribes paid to members of the selection committees. Among the disadvantaged youth, the exams become the new lodestone, a holy grail in which the bar for each year seems higher and more difficult to overcome. If passing the written test and interview and the declaration of his eligibility for the post of school headmaster boosted Mallesha's confidence, the long delay in receiving the appointment letter led to apprehension. Upset over the uncertainties and his state of unemployment, Mallesha fell ill. His old childhood illness of asthma and sinusitis returned. He spent nearly six weeks recuperating, and had to borrow money for his medical treatment.

After several months of waiting for information from the State Public Service Commission (nearly twenty-five months since he applied for the post), the despondent Mallesha returned to work as an independent signboard painter and a freelance artist. He got work only intermittently. His family relationships deteriorated. His mother expected him to get a full-time job and to cater to her and the daughter's family and their needs. He would have liked to join a non-profit organisation where his interest in art and education could be pursued, but his wife refused to work in a rural area. He now has a young son to look after as well, and his limited income is inadequate to cater to the growing family. He longs to be able to do creative work, to integrate art in education, and to read and write. But much of his daily life goes in preparing for exams, discussing strategies with friends, and working on hoardings and occasional painting jobs. Mallesha's condition is representative of the experience of many educated unemployed youth, which Craig Jeffrey (2010: 91) identifies as 'futureless waiting':

> a condition that marks the lives of millions of educated youth, who wait for jobs and appointments. Neither despondent nor wholly optimistic ... their openness to possibility can be glossed as a form of waiting that is neither straightforwardly purposeful nor purposeless but shares elements of both forms.

In seeking to make a transition from the world of a non-literate, informal economy to being recognised as an 'educated' and employable person aspiring to be a 'government employee', Mallesha experiences multiple forms of humiliation and degradation. It is not so much his failure or inability to have the 'capacity to aspire' (World Bank 2006) as much as the distortions created by the dominant model concerning the capabilities and skills that will enable him to be employed, and therefore become 'developed'. In the creation of an education–employment funnel that is narrow and limited, Mallesha remains marked as a 'failure', a man unable to gain the respect of his family and community. Craig Jeffrey (2010: 13) represents these experiences of the educated unemployed as

> ...a triple temporal hardship. First, they are unable to conform to dominant visions of how people should comport themselves with respect to linear, clock time—they 'miss years' or have 'gaps' on their resumes.... Second, they are unable to obtain the social goods, such as a secure white-collar job, which connote development.... Third, they are incapable of moving into gendered, age-based categories, especially male adulthood, such that they come to be labeled or label themselves as 'dropouts', 'failures' or people on the shelf.

Even as dominant discourse and theories recognise the multiple complexities and nuances of inequities such as 'durable inequalities' (Tilly 1998), inequalities of opportunities, and the persistence of the 'poverty trap', there is a lack of recognition of the hegemony of the dominant model and its imprint on the life-worlds of those it seeks to integrate into its system. The inability to gain entry into this dominant model and its system becomes a marker of failure and of the reproduction of the multiple forms of inequities, especially for the disadvantaged. As a hegemonic model that privileges only one trajectory for life and recognition, it becomes the basis for the erosion of the plural life-worlds of the disadvantaged. In experiencing this loss of the plurality of life-worlds and in the subsequent marking of those who have 'failed' (through competitive exams or through their inability to have the criteria of passing/gaining certification) lies the reproduction of a generation of people who stand as eroded and as 'wasted' (Bauman 2004). The impact of the presence of the educated unemployed on families, communities, and on the larger society has not been adequately understood or represented. Only a few scholars have pointed to the implications of such prolonged unemployment for intergenerational and gendered relationships which, in many cases, lead to the possibility of tension in marriages, and the increased risk of such youths, in the absence of gainful employment, becoming members of caste-based or religious associations, which often carry out communally motivated violence (Chowdhry 2010).

Mallesha—talented, sensitive, intelligent, and sincere— stands as a test case for the millions who are only known in official language as the 'educated unemployed', a category of persons who must either be retrained or refitted to suit a new economy and its new orientations. What Mallesha experiences as loss—of being unable to pursue his own interest and skills in fine arts, of being subjected to a process that demeans his worth and abilities, of gaining certain 'capabilities' (such as degrees, clearing government entrance exams) despite the very arduous process, and which in reality do not serve his own needs and desires—are issues that do not translate into objective, measurable criteria. Mainstream discourses in policy-planning and the deployment of agendas and programmes mostly recognise only those inequalities that can be addressed through a provisioning of education, health, access to resources, and, more recently, to a range of rights.[17] What of the hidden forms of exclusion which, in the apparent rhetoric of rights dissemination, capability development, and collective welfare orientation, impact the very foundation of the erosion of individuals? It would neither be right nor easy to say that Mallesha's life-world could have been drawn on the world of his ancestors, and that a life of being 'the shepherds-cum-leather workers' would have been a more suitable or better world for him. The limitations and depredations of such a world have been too well-elucidated for any serious consideration of seeking to return to caste-based occupations. But what marks Mallesha's life is not only the inability to realise himself, but also the stigma of being a failure despite having the certification that should have assured him success. He, like so many others in his cohort, is the bearer of the loaded promise of development, which in its unilinear and universalistic directives is increasingly a crucible in which the life, opportunities, and being of so many are tested.

In being removed from a life-world of knowledge and skills that were drawn from his family and caste background and further denied the ability to realise his own interests, and in being measured against the dominant paradigm of being 'developed', Mallesha experiences multiple dislocations and humiliations. Such subjection and disorientation by the larger system also denude Mallesha and his compatriots of a sense of agency and creates another circle of 'inequalities of agency' (Rao and Walton 2004). Subscribing to the dominant narrative and directives of being 'developed' and seeking legitimacy through it, Mallesha and his friends do not seek to critique, challenge, or disregard the system of education, examination, and job allocation. Instead, the long periods of waiting, preparation, and strategising to gain government employment make them passive participants in the system, and they also seek to play the system at its own game.[18] This alone accounts for their silence despite the long years of stress, open violation of codes of conduct, and the questionable methods in which the much sought after jobs are allocated.

Mallesha's background of multiple class/caste and cultural disadvantage, compounded by the social scarring by modern institutions and his own inability to fully comprehend or challenge it, represents a form of 'hermeneutical injustice', which Miranda Fricker (2011: 42) describes as '... the injustice of having some significant area of one's social experience obscured from collective understanding owing to persistent and wide-ranging hermeneutical marginalization'. His life and its tribulations represent the tensions of being caught between the disadvantages of a family, a community, and a regime of rights and development programmes which fails to address the very fundamental bases of inequality. Located within the very contradictions of a system that seeks to alter him and his life conditions, and yet retains him within its complex of disadvantages, Mallesha internalises the very norms of the larger apparatus and seeks to negotiate it on its own terms. The impact of this on Mallesha is personal and significant. He becomes subjected to the processes of submission, co-option, and compromise. The limitations of the macro-structures and their apparatus of institutions, processes, and rules mark the life-world of an individual who is also labelled as an 'educated unemployed'. Much of the outer promises of the agenda and programmes of mass and inclusive education then become forms of new sources of inequalities. For every outer promise made by the larger system (such as the government, projects/policies, other agencies), there is increasingly an inner denial (in the form of dysfunctional institutions, or forms of humiliation inherent in them which fail to recognise the potential of the students).

In 2014, close to ten years after I had first met him and started discussing his education and employment issues, I visited Mallesha at his home. He had finally been appointed as a high school headmaster (four years and ten months after his application) in a remote village (to which he commuted daily). He said that he did not find satisfaction in his job. Being a headmaster entailed primarily bureaucratic work, and he rarely got to teach. Yet, I observed a sort of newfound assurance about himself. And, as he noted, he was now recognised by his family and his fellow caste persons.

> I am now an official and part of the government. People recognise me for that. One cannot have what one would have liked ... a job doing what one likes. For people like us, being accepted (*sweekara*) and recognised (*guruthu*) by what society expects rather than being ourselves becomes our life's path. My path has also been like that.

NOTES

Acknowledgements: This paper was developed in 2017 as part of the German Historical Institute, London's Transnational Research Group's (TRG) project on 'Poverty and Education in India' and was a Working Paper in their series (see Vasavi 2017).

1. 'Mallesha' is a pseudonym, but all other details are factual. In 2004, Mallesha joined a research-cum- advocacy project that I was co-coordinating. In 2005, I noted his interest in applying for government jobs and we discussed his skills and interests, family life and pressures, etc., and I requested him to keep a diary. The

research project closed in 2007, but we remained in contact and he visited me often in Bengaluru. I was privy to his struggles to focus on his art and education work, and yet gain entry into a government job. In 2009, when he quit his job, I provided him with occasional financial support, and he worked in a research project but was unable to commit to being a full-time member. In 2010, we reviewed his diary and notes, and I reframed several questions. We followed the details of the case of the recruitment of headmasters, both through his personal experiences and through discussions and reports in the press. In writing this chapter, I have translated selections from his diary (written in Kannada), and shared the draft versions of the chapter with him. He approved the chapter in its entirety, but requested the use of a pseudonym for his name.

2. The term 'Scheduled Caste' is drawn from the official schedule which identifies persons from former 'untouchable castes', and also from other low-ranked caste groups, who are entitled to a range of government-based protective measures. The term has now gained social currency and many of these groups use it to identify themselves as 'Scheduled Caste', or use the abbreviation 'SC' rather than the term 'Dalit'.
3. An autobiography (first published in Kannada and then translated into English) by Aravind Malagatti (1994), called *Government Brahmana*, refers to such labelling. But the label is widely and covertly used by upper-caste students and faculty to refer to reserved category students and employees (including faculty). Such labelling and name-calling increased after the anti-reservation agitations, also called the Anti-Mandal agitation, in 1990.
4. Estimates for the number of youth in India vary, depending on the definition of youth. Currently, based on a definition of youth as ranging from 15–24 years, there are approximately 240 million youth (GoI 2014) who constitute the world's largest body of youth. Of these, only about 20 per cent make it to high school and only about 11 per cent up to the college or university level. Numbers for educated unemployed also vary, but reliable assessments indicate it to be around 6.5 million (see Dev and Venkatanarayana 2011).
5. B. R. Ambedkar referred to 'graded inequality' as a specific form of caste-based inequality in which hierarchical caste ranking and ordering meant that each caste was relatively unequal to those above it.
6. Although this may be seen as representing a form of 'para-ethnography' (see Holmes and Marcus 2005), I do not draw from this genre of

social anthropology. Instead, I draw on the use of diaries and frequent discussions with the interlocutor, along with observations of structuring issues and public debates, as a form of engaged fieldwork in which anthropological questions of not only culture but also structures (and their political economies), and the agency, voice, and representation of the subject are sought to be addressed.

7. Göran Therborn (2009) identifies three types of inequalities: 'vital inequalities' that pertain to inequalities of health and death; 'existential inequalities' which mark individuals and marginal groups; and 'resource and material inequalities'.
8. Madigas (also spelt as Maadigas or Maadhigas) were originally associated with leather (or handling dead cows) and are akin to the north Indian group of Chamars, the Madigas of Andhra Pradesh, and the Chakliyars of Tamil Nadu. In Karnataka, they account for the second highest proportion of SCs and are considered 'untouchables' by many caste groups. As a group that has taken to various non-caste occupations, the Madigas of Karnataka are relatively well-organised in terms of political mobilisation, and are now seeking special quotas for themselves within the caste-based reservation system. Those who are organised now subscribe to the 'Dalit' identity and assertions that mark many of the Madiga youth associations.
9. The Jomtien Conference was first held in 1990, and India was a signatory to this conference. Many of the recent directives for elementary education have been set by the terms of the Jomtien Conference.
10. Mathas are Hindu religious orders established and run by various sects. Many have spiritual leaders who are seen as both religious and temporal leaders (relating to the domains of politics and economy).
11. See Weisskopf (2004) for a comprehensive overview of the limitations of the affirmative action programme in the US and India. See also Deshpande (2011) for an argument that contextualises the tension between the new trends in the growing privatisation of education, and the continued demand and need for affirmative action programmes in education. Although Rohith Vemula's suicide at the University of Hyderabad in 2016, and the nationwide agitations called 'Justice for Rohith' (see *Hindustan Times* 2016; *The Wire* 2019) brought to public notice and debate the extant discrimination, neglect, and humiliation that reserved category students experience in higher education institutions, no substantial changes have been made in the education institutional cultures.

12. Bögenhold elaborates on Blossfeld and Shavit's work in thirteen different countries, which found that rapid educational expansion did not reduce inequalities of educational opportunities. They concluded:

    As a consequence of educational expansion, societies can produce a higher average level of educational attainment from one birth cohort to the next, without changing the educational opportunities of children from different social strata.... Thus, the modernisation theorists' hypothesis of educational opportunities must be turned on its head: expansion actually facilitates to a large extent the persistence of inequalities in educational opportunity (as cited by Bögenhold 2001: 838).

13. These are periodic examinations conducted by state governments to recruit persons into government posts. Large numbers (up to a quarter of a million sometimes) of aspiring candidates undertake these exams and wait for long periods for the final selection to be conducted.
14. The State Public Services Commission is responsible for the recruitment of all government employees. While the process is supposedly open and examination-based, the biases and corruption enter at the time of interviews, for which a substantial proportion of marks is allocated. In addition, in recent years, allegations of corruption in the very constitution of the board of members of the Public Services Commission have made the legitimacy of the Commission dubious.
15. H. N. Krishna, Chairman of the Karnataka Public Services Commission (KPSC), along with three others, was indicted by the Criminal Investigation Department (CID) for irregularities and illegalities in the recruitment of public servants in the years 1998, 1999, and 2004. After filing charges, he was arrested in October 2011 and imprisoned before being granted bail. See *The Hindu* (2011, 2021a, 2021b) and *Deccan Herald* (2011).
16. See *Education World* (2021) for the conflict between teachers' associations and the new recruits.
17. India has, over the past few years, been implementing a range of rights. While the Right to Information (RTI) (2005) and the Right to (Elementary) Education (RTE) bills have been passed more recently (August 2009), a range of bills pertaining to rights to food and housing are on the anvil. This is in addition to the establishment of

a number of commissions to safeguard and promote human rights. As critics have pointed out, the promulgation of these rights, which have gained currency in discourses of governmentality, are ironically matched by a decline in the functioning of public institutions meant to safeguard or ensure these rights.

18. Common friends alleged that Mallesha had, along with some of his neighbourhood friends, bribed one of the interviewers to guarantee him the job. When I discussed this with Mallesha, he denied it. So I am unable to ascertain whether this took place or not.

VI

REFLEXIVE AND RELATIONAL, EMPATHETIC AND ENGAGED

A Case for 'Social Transformative Learning' in India

In the search for alternatives and new directions in addressing the problems and the perpetual state of crisis of India's universities, we have to assert the need for new imaginaries, categories, and practices in education. In multiple ways, a highly differentiated and differentiating educational system is creating disjunctions in the learning, capability, orientation, and aspirations of our citizens. These include the contradictory marking of youth with alienation from their provenance while at the same time integrating them into the narrow cultures of closed reference groups (that is, cultures with narrow agendas which act as their own reference group), fostering the idea that the primary objective of university education is to seek formal employment, and thereby missing the objectives of forming a broader mind and intellect and disengaging youth from the processes, institutions, and structures of public and democratic responsibility, instead integrating them into the circuits of consumer capitalism and mass popular culture. The failure of the university to be a democratic entity and encouraging the internalisation of a culture and ethos of democracy has enabled multiple forms of reproduction of inequalities. Rather than a focus on fostering 'development'-oriented programmes, there is an urgency to initiate and institute a broad-based culture of democracy through which the reproduction of structures of privilege (for the dominant) and the culture of submission (of the subordinated) can be halted. While these aspects can be the benchmark for a re-addressal of universities and their functioning and orientation, there are several challenges which require specific responses and strategies.

Concentrating on the need for transformative learning rather than reproductive education, this chapter provides two broad perspectives. First, the limitations of higher education in India are identified and the potential of Social Transformative Learning (STL) is elaborated. Second, based on a broad overview of some existing ideas on STL, some key issues in the development of STL for India are identified.

INTERROGATING THE INDIAN UNIVERSITY: THE NEED FOR STL IN INDIA

Amidst the explosion of higher educational institutions and the focus on career options and competitiveness, there is the need to engage with students to provide a broader definition of education. One such approach can be 'Social Transformative Learning', or STL, which can facilitate critical thinking and the social capabilities of learners. In the Indian context, where higher education has typically meant the reproduction of the dominant structures of society; where issues of caste, class, gender, and religious differences evade general understanding; and where commonsensical opinions have greater influence than informed ideas, there is a pressing need to integrate STL into post-school or university education. While there is a substantial body of literature on STL in the Western context, the possibilities of promoting this in the Indian context can be considered. Given the moribund conditions of higher education institutions in the nation, there is an urgency to initiate programmes in which STL can be the core. A particular challenge concerns the question: How can learners be transformed into reflexive, critical thinkers who can engage with the range of situations found in their society and in the nation?

Rendered primarily as a 'parking lot' in which the youth[1] in large numbers spend the best part of their young lives (ages 18 to 24 or so), the average institution of higher education/university in India is mired in problems. The recent push to expand higher education has not been a genuine effort to address issues of exclusion, but a policy that has turned mass education into a political alibi. Further, the university is unable to 'identify institutional fulcrums around which a new world can be fashioned with progress and reform. Thus universities have become "duckback" institutions over which new ideas and reforms roll off' (Moosvi 2012). Even as there is the push to expand,[2] primarily to meet international comparative figures in terms of enrolment, the university as an institution is beset with multiple problems: an inability to function as a model democratic institution or to inculcate a sense of respect for the world of ideas; a failure to engage students in the worlds of updated knowledge; the contradiction of alienating students from their provenance and social backgrounds/livelihoods and yet rendering them unemployable and unsuitable for the new global economy; and the reproduction of dominant structures of hierarchy, discrimination, and exclusion.

Directives from 'think tanks' such as the National Knowledge Commission (NKC)[3] have led to the establishment of universities that actually defy the idea of the 'university' itself. The growing specialisation has meant that universities have moved far away from becoming comprehensive centres of knowledge. Universities for petroleum, dentistry, law, etc., are now being established by both the government and private edu-entrepreneurs as standalone institutions which not only challenge ideas of the 'university', but also erode any possibility of their emerging as 'multiversities'. Such trends also imply the rendering of universities into arenas of the 'edu-factory',[4] whereby knowledge is increasingly entrenched in capitalist production and accumulation, and is further reintegrated into capitalist circuits by the subordination of learners into the new hierarchies of labour. Government schemes, which lead to the establishment of institutions that cater to populist demands and are not necessarily attended by assurances of quality, result in many new institutions that are increasingly failing to meet the basic standards of what a comprehensive university or higher education institution could mean. A case in point is the government's intent to establish new universities for 'religious minorities',[5] an idea that will only reinforce the insularity of educational experience. Such populist education expansion is matched by the growing privatisation of education, in which age-old forms of exclusion are being reinforced. While the denial of equal opportunity to deserving and economically disadvantaged students continues, the alliance between the university and the industry is also manifesting varied forms of distortions. These include the relegation of social sciences and humanities, the excessive emphasis on employment-oriented courses, and an overall disengagement from comprehensive education.

Although the policy of 'positive discrimination' or 'reservations' has enabled a sizeable number of students from disadvantaged family and caste backgrounds to gain entry into the university, the impact of the education system on them is yet to be seen as being 'positive'. While large numbers remain unemployed and their political awareness remains deficient, the gains to such disadvantaged communities stay limited. Decades of indifference has meant that there is an absence of critical thinking. This includes the neglect of B. R. Ambedkar's emancipatory ideology as a whole, as Ambedkar was until recently, largely recognised as a historical icon mainly among circles of Dalit activists, and is only lately being recognised as a major socio-political thinker. Perhaps what is most striking about the impact of mainstream education on the body of disadvantaged students is its failure to address the long-term 'social scarring' that such students have experienced, and the compounding of such marginalisation by poor quality education. This marginalisation is reflected in an absence of understanding vis-à-vis the social contexts of Dalit lives, which lack social capital (that most upper-caste members enjoy), and the fact that most Dalit students embody and represent forms of 'subjected personhood'.[6] Such 'subjected personhood' refers to 'personalities and orientations in which there is an erosion of agency, and the self-worth of individuals and/or groups is not individually defined or directed but is marked by the violence of persistent and pervasive humiliation, deprivation and indignities' (Vasavi 2006a: 376). These markers on most Dalit students are augmented by the socialisation and the internalisation of caste norms, which have led to a typical submission to hegemonic forms of discrimination and exploitation.

The failure of the Indian university is also evident when it is assessed in terms of its contribution to regional or site-specific issues and problems. Even so-called regional universities, set up to cater to various regions, are merely poor clones of the larger universities; they act as 'certification' or exam centres and do not provide region-specific knowledge, know-how, or skills. For example, none of the regional universities provide courses or training that can pertain to the specific socio-economic, agricultural, ecological, architectural, and medical requirements of different regions. Even as regional universities remain poor second cousins to the metropolitan and central universities, the new universities meant to cater to specific disadvantaged groups suffer the same problems. One glaring example of this mindless cloning of universities without attention to the needs of the clientele population is that of the 'tribal' or Adivasi university at Amarkantak in Madhya Pradesh (Indira Gandhi National Tribal University, or IGNTU), which lacks any imagination towards catering to the needs of tribals. Instead, the university offers mostly mainstream courses with a few 'tribal or anthropological studies' thrown in.[7]

States such as Chhattisgarh and Jharkhand, primarily inhabited by Adivasis, require a pool of region-specific knowledge so as to be 'developed' in ecologically and socio-culturally specific ways. However, there is an absence of such knowledge-generating initiatives and ideas. Instead, there is a rampant mimicry of outdated and irrelevant 'development' programmes that only legitimise the further degradation of these areas and the local population. This is only one glaring example of the failure of regional universities.

Since knowledge creation, teaching, research, and publications remain tied to received paradigms of Western scholarship (but largely without the average standards or creativity of these models), there is a deep sense of disengagement from the 'vicinity'.[8] The 'vicinity' (beyond the identification of the local) refers to an area or region with a specific socio-historical background and ecological specificities, which is impacted by its linkages to larger socio-economic and political forces. Living in any specific vicinity requires understanding, relating to, and working in and on it on multiple levels, and education needs to factor in how to foster, develop, and focus on enabling the knowledge of different vicinities.

Perhaps the key limitation of the Indian university is its poor quality, which has rendered millions unemployable rather than merely unemployed. Such conditions mean the marking of youth as largely failures and rendering them unfit for either their own communities, especially those that are rural, agrarian, or crafts-based, or for the new economy. More particularly, in a context where the youth form a large pool of the population, this listlessness that results from unemployment, underemployment, and alienation is also the basis for the integration of youth into violent anti-social activities. Most of the perpetrators of the extant forms of violence that India has recently witnessed, such as lynching, raping, initiating mob violence, obstructing justice, and indulging in calumny and false news via the new social media, are primarily products of the poor and disorienting mass higher education system. Among those who do manage to succeed through the processes and markers of examinations, university education does not typically provide the perspectives, skills, and scope to become engaged and informed citizens. The reproduction of inherited or received ideas, especially those about privilege and notions of merit, continues to constitute the commonsensical thinking of a majority of educated people. This has been blatantly visible in the hostility that a majority of students displayed during the turbulent period of 'Anti-Mandal' agitation.[9] In addition, the recent mobilisation of large bodies of youth into extremist politics and violent organisations is a troubling trend which requires attention. Overall, the expansion of the higher education system in India, based primarily on enabling access and matching international figures, without attention to the content, orientation, impact, and specificities of India's needs, has meant that there is what W. E. B. Du Bois identified as 'systemic miseducation'.[10]

In summary, the limitations of the dominant education system in India are the following:

1. Mainstream education is based on received and dominant ideas, and the regurgitation and reproduction of dominant ideas is often the marker of successful 'education'.
2. In a hierarchical and layered society such as India with its range of institutions and programmes (that are also differentially aligned), the impact on the marginalised and disadvantaged youth is such that they are forced to fit in and are domesticated into the mainstream economy and culture, where they continue to occupy either subordinate positions, or have become part of reproducing the larger socio-cultural apparatus.
4. In the context of the increasing marketisation of education and of fitting learners into the market model (as employees), the effect on the individual, the society, and the nation has been detrimental, eroding the abilities of educated youth to be engaged citizens, and/or to be reflexive members of their societies.
5. Given the overall limitations of the mainstream education system, there is a need for new paradigms and perspectives in education, so that both individual abilities and collective responsibilities can be enhanced.

Given such trends and results, the challenge in India is to go beyond the rhetoric of access and inclusion, and focus on ways to facilitate educational justice. Some foundational shifts that are required to challenge the deep and multiple morasses that beset higher education in India are the following:

(*i*) A rethink on the idea of 'higher education' and the institutions, processes, and markers of legitimacy associated with being educated;

(*ii*) Shifting from an excessively formal system (in which certification and state-approved norms are key) to facilitating a range of learning contexts and engagements which can be legitimised. Even initiating such a process will require the creation of a pool of resource persons (and not just as teachers) who can act as facilitators and as catalysts for social transformation;

(*iii*) In terms of educational philosophy, pedagogies, and approaches, a substantial shift towards enabling an affective and emotive scaffolding of learners will first have to be made. Contrary to mainstream education, such alternative learning forms will have to bridge the gap between the worlds of formal learning and that of society, and draw on the multiple knowledge forms and skills that remain informal epistemes;

(*iv*) In addition, going beyond the idea of simply reviving local knowledge forms, new and integrative knowledge that can address the limitations of both local knowledge forms and that of the formal systems need to be emphasised. More particularly, the challenge of replacing the dominant structures of power, knowledge, and relationships will have to be made the cornerstone of such endeavours.

Alternative Education and Attempts at Social Transformative Learning (STL)

Over the past few decades, especially since the 1970s, there have been a few endeavours at initiating STL in India. Although none of these have consciously or deliberately adopted or drawn on the term, the focus on facilitating change, on questioning the status quo, and the attempt to empower the disadvantaged have been their key objectives. Since the 1970s, there have been several attempts at introducing Paulo Freire's ideas and thoughts, but these have been restricted to small alternative groups and endeavours. A key problem that has resulted in Freirean methods remaining either restricted to certain circles or to being domesticated and appropriated (without their attendant significance and impact) is linked to its co-option by large mission-mode programmes, such as that of the National Literacy Mission. The lack of availability of a large pool of trained resource persons, the failure to develop localised pedagogies and texts, and the dilution and simplification of Freirean methods have meant that the latter has not really made significant inroads into critical pedagogies. Other institution-based efforts include alternative educational programmes and institutions from various states such as Eklavya (Madhya Pradesh), Shikshantar (Rajasthan), Vidyodaya (Tamil Nadu), Vidya Ashram (Varanasi), and Tulir (Tamil Nadu), which have sought to initiate critical thinking and pedagogies at the school and post-school levels. The Jesuits' attempt over the years to provide an 'Option for the Poor'[11] has also been an effort that has systematically sought to include disadvantaged communities into the educational agenda; they have also extended Jesuit institutions to areas which serve the disadvantaged.

One other effort, at the post-graduate level, is that of the Centre for Research and Education in Social Transformation (CREST) in Kozhikode, Kerala. A brief overview[12] of its approach and impact will indicate the possibilities of STL.

CREST, Kozhikode, Kerala

'How can disadvantaged students be supported so as to enable them to compete in the fast globalising world and in the private sector?' This is CREST's key orientation, and since 2002, when it was established by the Government of Kerala in collaboration with the Indian Institute of Management (IIM), Kozhikode (Kerala), it has emerged as one of India's primary institutions catering to graduate students from scheduled communities of the state. In setting up the institution, the government's objectives were focused on enabling students from such communities to gain entry into private-sector employment and/or to higher and professional education, including entry into international institutions and universities. CREST has broadened this objective further to provide an enabling learning experience for its students.

CREST's vision is expressed as follows: 'To move towards new horizons of creating a just, equitable and caring society through empowerment of the marginalised and underprivileged sections based on the principles of humanism, equality and social justice.' CREST's mission is stated to be:

> To facilitate the marginalised and the underprivileged to gain confidence, build competence and achieve excellence in all spheres of human endeavour, for their social, cultural and economic development through education, training, and research and consulting. Its specific objectives included helping SC/ST candidates to compete in the open market for admission/jobs in institutions/organisations of repute as well as assisting them to compete as research and development scholars. It also provides training to improve the competence of members of scheduled communities while working in the organised sector (Nampoothiri 2011: 7).

The faculty face several challenges while working with the students, many of whom have low aspiration levels, feel defeated by the larger competitive world, and lack confidence and communication skills (with limited abilities in English). In addition, their generally low socio-economic status means that the students face pressure to secure immediate employment, which in many cases do not match their aptitude or skills. Taking all these factors into consideration, the CREST faculty has evolved a programme whose pedagogies include the following:

1. Participative learning;
2. Interactive learning processes;
3. Real-life experiential learning;
4. Activity-based classrooms;
5. Learning through fun by using relevant games, etc.;
6. Simulative learning through role plays, skits, and theatrical methods.

Identifying these pedagogies, one of the faculty members notes that

> the above-mentioned methodologies are used to help the students to communicate and share their experiences, inadequacies, fears, etc., and connect them with issues of religion, caste, creed, gender, morale, self esteem, and culture. Based on the progress of each session, the trainer is able to discuss and address individual and group issues. The process is cathartic and self-healing. This leads to a fair degree of emotional maturity in problem-solving.[13]

In addition to these, CREST faculty has occasionally had to provide extra psychological counselling to students who have experienced traumatic and disturbing events in their personal lives.

Responses and evaluations from alumni indicate that CREST has been a significant life-changing experience for them. As one of them once told me, it was the first time in her life that she had been asked what she wanted, rather than being told what to do. In addition to gaining confidence and skills in relating to the larger world, the focus on understanding and recognising the history and trends in their own communities has provided an important empathetic factor in their learning. One student, now an alumna, described her recognition of her own community as follows:

> Though I am a Scheduled Tribe (Mala Arayan), I had never gone deep into the details of the community. But the self-actualisation module at CREST gave us an opportunity to know more about our own communities. We had to interview elderly people from our own community, which enabled me to know more. There were people who really came out successful from hardships, but there were also people who still are bound to an attitude of not changing for the better.[14]

Another alumnus pointed out that realisation of caste-based differences and of the impact of the caste system on lower caste lives was significant for him: 'My attitude to my community and society had a major impact after CREST…I started thinking about unprivileged people in my society and community.'

The programme and teaching-learning initiatives at CREST have been enabling the students, and have charted the possibility of endowing them with skills and capabilities with which to engage with the larger dominant world. Given the state (Kerala) government's mandate of supporting Scheduled community students to gain entry into the private and professional sectors, the focus has been primarily on providing training and orientation for professional development and facilitating entry into private-sector industries or careers. While much of the training seems to have made a significant impact on the students, thus enabling them to accrue those skills and capabilities that can assist them to compete in employment arenas, much more needs to be done to enable the students to emerge as engaged and proactive citizens. The limited time (the course period is only four months) is a handicap, and CREST is only able to transact some basic skills and capabilities. Much more time is required to enable the students to be more 'socially transformed'. This may also be the key reason why so far, none of the alumni has been engaged in public work or in politics. Instead, the success stories or successful students are identified as those who have been able to gain entry into either the corporate sector, higher educational institutions, or become independent entrepreneurs. Perhaps CREST's key contribution is its ability to challenge the key markers of inferiority, inadequacy, and insecurity among disadvantaged students.

If CREST has been able to initiate some work in the arena of transformative education, then more attention needs to be paid to developing a comprehensive education programme that can be integrated into education at all levels (elementary and high school, and higher and professional education), and which can also address the challenge of initiating change among privileged students.

Social Transformative Learning for Privileged Students

It would be inadequate to consider STL as being appropriate only for learners or students from disadvantaged backgrounds. Instead, given that the source of the reproduction of any unequal and unjust society lies among the privileged, it is important that STL also be extended to them. Challenging their assumptions, prejudices, and biases requires new modes of unlearning and relearning. Given that in most cases privileged students and youth tend to be subject to what Friere considered to be the 'anesthetization of the mind' (Van Gorder 2008: 2), and are enveloped in structures and cultures of privilege, there is a need to deploy pedagogies that can question such privilege and their taken-for-granted terms of reference. That there is a need to include the privileged into the ambit of STL is also highlighted by Van Gorder (ibid: 5), who points out that:

> Education for the privileged is not interested in promoting an awareness of the 'invasive nature' of social injustice. The privileged, in fact, are encouraged to see themselves in a positive light as those who are deeply concerned about the plight of those they are actually responsible (directly or indirectly) for tyrannizing. The privileged protect their status as superior while also paternalistically thinking of themselves (in the context of Western societies) as the 'great White hope' of benighted, oppressed people who are in need of their assistance....

Enabling oppressors or the privileged to question their complicity in the reproduction of inequity will also require the Freirean methods of conscientisation, problematisation, and reflexivity. In addition to this, patriarchal, institutionalised, or religiously-ordained ideas prevent a recognition of the structures and processes by which domination is naturalised and taken for granted.

In the context of India, where the focus has primarily been on a simplistic reproduction of the dominant system and where only a few alternative endeavours have focused on the disadvantaged, it may be opportune to consider including and developing a specialised STL for advantaged students/learners. Key methodologies and orientations, especially those suitable for a range of contexts in India, are yet to be worked out, but the need and potential are immense. Combining the need to address both the social and emotional scarring that socio-economic disadvantage leaves, and the social myopia that cultures of privilege endow the rich with, it may be appropriate to review the potential of STL to address these two divergent groups of learners.

Social Transformative Learning: An Overview of Existing Literature and Debates

> *Social Transformative Learning is a theory of deep learning that goes beyond just content knowledge acquisition, or learning equations, memorising tax codes or learning historical facts and data. It is a desirable process for adults to learn to think for themselves, through true emancipation from sometimes mindless or unquestioning acceptance of what we have come to know through our life experience, especially those*

> *things that our culture, religions, and personalities may predispose us towards, without our active engagement and questioning of how we know what we know* (Mezirow et al. 2000: 20).

Although recognised as a founding father of STL, Jack Mezirow's perspectives on STL, developed since 1975, have drawn on earlier thinkers such as Paulo Freire and others. Focusing on adult learning, Mezirow called for an emphasis on contextual understanding, critical reflection on assumptions, and validated meaning by assessing reasons. These were to enable adults to not only critically review their own roles, but also to develop 'self-authorship', both for their own lives and to be able to contribute to their societies. Patricia Cranton, another leading writer on transformative learning, defines it to include the idea of people changing the way they interpret their experiences and their interactions with the world. This includes the ways in which 'an individual becomes aware of holding a limiting or distorted view. If the individual critically examines this view, opens herself to alternatives, and consequently changes the way she sees things, she has transformed some part of how she makes meaning out of the world' (Cranton 2006: 2). For Mezirow, this transformation of perspective included going through the following ten ordered phases (as listed by Cranton [ibid.: 20]):

1. Experiencing a disorienting dilemma;
2. Undergoing self-examination;
3. Conducting a critical assessment of internalised assumptions, and feeling a sense of alienation from traditional social expectations;
4. Relating discontent to the similar experiences of others—recognising that the problem is shared;
5. Exploring options for new ways of acting;
6. Building competence and self-confidence in new roles;
7. Planning a course of action;
8. Acquiring the knowledge and skills for implementing a new course of action;
9. Trying out new roles and assessing them;
10. Reintegrating into society with the other perspective.

To summarise Mezirow, this 'perspective transformation' is 'a structural change in the way we see ourselves and our relationships' (Mezirow 1978: 100). More importantly, it is the process of effecting change in a 'frame of reference' that is central to initiating transformational learning. In focusing on the need for a change in the reference framework, and in allowing for processes that are also context-specific, STL offers a viable approach to initiate new learning paradigms and practices in India. While much of what has happened to Freirean methods, such as co-option, is also tenable here, it is also pertinent for educationists to contextually assess each of these methods.

STL for the Indian Context

What are the frames of reference in the Indian context that require change? Can the reference shift from the individual to the collective? What should this collective be? In a context where a combination of ideas of individualism (relating to work, market, and ambition) are anchored within a frame of collective identity (family, community, caste, and religion), what alternative is required to facilitate STL for an equitable and just society? The challenge is to interrogate the dominant systems so that the myriad existing problems of hierarchy and inequity are addressed, and the pressing need to turn learning into a pathway leading to a new worldview and to a new world is emphasised. In this search, the emphasis should be on making self-transformation the cornerstone of STL so that social or macro changes can be initiated via the individual. Given the cultures of discrimination and exploitation, there must be an emphasis on self-recognition and enabling. For both groups, the disadvantaged and the privileged, the objectives should be to overcome both the culture of silence and the culture of privilege, which also includes the fact that many privileged persons suffer from what education philosopher, Deepti Mehrotra[15] has identified as 'afflictions of affluence'. These are evident in the problems that economically privileged people exhibit (such as lack of initiative, taking existing systems for granted, inability to foster alternative ideas, etc.), and which hinder their own personal growth as well as that of the society. Addressing this in conjunction with the hardships that economically and socially disadvantaged persons experience requires an educational system that ensures that every individual has a voice, agency, and representation. As with the Freirean methods, for Social Transformative Learning to take place, the pedagogies of questioning, dialogue, critical thinking, and conscientisation need to be asserted. The linkages between the individual, the family, the community or neighbourhood, and the larger society and nation need to be explicated and contextualised.

If the above are the broad approaches to STL in India, some of the key methods that need to be further developed with clarity on themes, pedagogies, texts, and processes relate to the four key perspectives, discussed in the following section. For STL to be promoted, educationists should consider ways to draw on these four frames while developing teaching-learning programmes for all disciplines and the themes within them.

Issues and Themes in STL

Reflexive/Reflexivity: How can all themes/topics incorporate reflexivity as part of pedagogies? Here, reflexivity is defined as the ability to rethink or question issues. It includes critically rethinking inherited cultures and traditions and taken-for-granted frames of reference. For example: Can we identify a range of contexts (in the everyday and in special events) in which hierarchy is assumed, and what are its implications?

Can the caste system and class relations be explicated as a system of hierarchy? Instead of a formal analytical overview, can everyday issues of hierarchy (at home, in school, at work, in public and private lives) be unpacked? Can learners be made aware of the impact of hierarchical thinking on their lives?

Relational/Relationality: Can the relationships between persons and groups, and between disciplines and themes, between objects and persons, between worlds, and between ideas be explicated? Can the relationships between past and present, present and future be laid out? Can interlinks between different domains (physical, social, and economic worlds) be made explicit? For example: Can the relationship between low pay and the lack of bargaining power be made explicit? Can the impact of consumerism on the environment be made recognisable?

Empathetic/Empathy: Can sensitivity towards others (persons, animals, worlds, groups) be made central? How can a person place herself/himself in the shoes of another? What worlds do those who are subordinated or disadvantaged occupy? For example: What if a learner is made to follow all the rules that a working-class Dalit is subject to? Can a male learner be made to act and follow all the restrictions that a typical woman of his age would be forced to subscribe to?

Engaged/Engagement: Can the learning sessions provide for the engagement of all learners' skills and abilities in the everyday world that they inhabit? Engagement should include abilities to interact with structures, processes, and agencies/agents of power and disempowerment. For example: What are the ways in which learners can improve their own environment (not only physical, but also social)? What key social issue can they engage in as part of their everyday civic work, or in contexts of pressing issues that need addressal? What changes or differences can they initiate in their everyday lives?

The key objectives of STL should be to evolve perspectives, methodologies, pedagogies, and texts which can go beyond the standard and mainstream approaches of knowledge transfer, and facilitate the questioning of the dominant society and its cultures. Going beyond the established transactions of classroom-based teaching and examinations, a new portfolio of standards and processes must be implemented. These can include both site/place-based projects and the studies which build on new pedagogies and teaching-learning transactions that emphasise reflexive, relational, empathetic, and engaged learning.

In addition to the above, there are several 'details' which need to be worked out, especially for the Indian context. Other approaches to complement ideas from both Freirean methods and STL are to consider ways in alternative learning for rural youth. Drawing on the orientations of 'place-based education',[16] critical thinking, social transformative learning, and integrated knowledge may be ways to overcome many of the limitations of mainstream education, especially that of post-school education. In working with youth from disadvantaged backgrounds, it is important to bear the following in mind:

1. With their histories of being subordinated by a larger system that sees them as less endowed, and the layered sense of inadequacy that many youth embody, it is important to consider ways to provide 'emotional scaffolding'. Such scaffolding should include the recognition of the larger systemic injustices which have marked them, an understanding of their collective histories (which can enable them to overcome their individualised biographies), and a sense of recognition of their self-worth. Instead of purely academic learning, the preliminary phase should focus on enabling each learner to emerge as a confident individual, recognising her/his abilities and interests, and with the skills to negotiate the various demands of a larger world. The ability to communicate well and be expressive will also be key.
2. Attention must be paid to the dynamics between different social/cultural groups, and therefore to the dynamics of the learning context and the reproduction of social tensions within the learning domain. Although segregated or homogenous student bodies are considered limiting, inasmuch as they do not provide for a socially inclusive form of learning, this may be reviewed in terms of the dynamics between two widely heterogenous groups. In contexts of clear-cut divisions and tensions among learners as 'dominant' vs. 'subordinate', it may be a challenge to enable the subordinate to overcome their diffidence and lack of confidence. In such situations, it may be preferable to have socially homogenous groups in which the pedagogies and transactions take into consideration the shared social backgrounds of the learners.
3. Learning programmes for disadvantaged youth need to recognise that livelihoods and a source of income are

pressing needs for the youth. Generalised learning or orientation programmes are not seen as attractive, and may be considered redundant to their immediate needs of economic security. In such contexts, STL needs to be embedded within programmes that provide livelihood skills. General/critical thinking or conscientisation and other social and political orientation drawn on STL can be built into livelihood skills and training.

4. There is also the additional and related challenge of preparing youth for either independent livelihoods, or for those that are linked to the market and entrepreneurship. What role and position does citizenship play in this context? Are the two incompatible, or should they be seen as interlinked, with obligations in one domain also being relevant in the other?

These are only some of the pressing issues that need to be borne in mind. In addition, much more attention needs to be paid to developing programmes in which the STL approach can be embedded into formal and informal types of education. Linkages between the themes (and not necessarily disciplines), texts or materials, pedagogies, assessment, etc., will also have to be deliberated upon and developed. More particularly, special attention will have to be paid to developing parameters or criteria for assessing learning, thereby going beyond standard academic performance (see Appendix I for alternative criteria). Issues of language, access, and interlinkages to the world of English will also have to be addressed in a manner that recognises language abilities as not only a means of communication, but also as a form of cultural capital. 'We change society by changing ourselves, and we change ourselves in our struggle to change society' (Mclaren 2009: 3).

The cornerstone of STL should surely be based on this rallying cry for linking education and social transformation. Education, as a process and an endeavour, and the institutions associated with it face multiple challenges. At a macro level, this includes the pressing urgency to rethink knowledge forms at a time of

'Great Disruption' (of the economic faltering of capitalism and the deepening ecological crisis) (Gilding 2011). Hence, there is need to rethink the very premises of several disciplines and to initiate new, interdisciplinary/integrated knowledge forms that can overcome the limitations of some of those that have become foundational sciences. At a more micro and interior level is the challenge of facilitating knowledge forms and educational skills that will enable the recognition of, and work according to ecological and social requirements, rather than catering to market demands.

There are multiple challenges in the mainstream education system that need to be addressed. These include the trend of rendering knowledge into 'new forms of educational capitalism that cultivate a new spirit of enterprise and the enterprise curriculum, giving a new emphasis to the entrepreneurial subject' (Peters 2009: 42). Such an orientation, which closely aligns with neoliberal policies of privatising and turning education into a commercial enterprise, is also compounded by new learning, and examination systems that are high-technology and market-oriented. In such contexts, there is the need to develop new curricula and outreach programmes so that the distantiation of the earlier knowledge and institutional regimes from myriad communities/societies, especially those that are marginal and disadvantaged, is overcome. The space and linkages that universities must interact with are both the 'vicinity' (not necessarily limited to the local) and the universal, where the specificities of the vicinity can be understood and catered to, while also engaging with and drawing on the validity of what has become universal. The vicinity must also act as the litmus test for validating the knowledge of the universal. Curricula and content of learning sources must both induct and deduct from the vicinity, the particular and the immediate to the universal (or generalisable level), so that varied localised innovations can be legitimised and disseminated.

The defining questions of the STL practices can centre around the following:

1. Have the voice and agency of the learner been scaffolded to enable her/him to be an active citizen?

2. How will the forms of knowledge transmitted to the learner facilitate her/his life, relations with the immediate community, and with the larger society and nation?
3. Will the knowledge forms pass the criteria of environmental, social, and economic audits in which sustainability is the key criteria? What implications do these knowledge forms have for the domains of the economy, polity, society, and ecology?
4. Does this knowledge enable both individual growth (in skills, knowledge, abilities) and the ability to contribute to collective responsibilities?

While the above are only generalised criteria, specific ones suitable to the themes, age, context, and social background of learners need to be evolved.

If the mainstream university as we know it now is no longer the beacon for constituting a pool of learned and engaged citizens, there is an urgent need to nudge it towards becoming a responsive institution, forging, integrating, and disseminating new knowledge forms, catering to new learners, and bridging the chasm between the formal world of learning and the life-worlds of myriad societies. Yet, the more significant challenge in developing an STL for India lies in the ability to answer the question Martin Buber posed long ago: 'For whom and for what is education?' And to also recognise the caveat that John Dewey posed: 'We will know what type of education to provide, if we know what type of society we want.' It may only be in our ability to respond to these two challenges that a comprehensive education system can be evolved, and in this, STL may be one small step.

NOTES

1. Although only about 11–12 per cent of the cohort of 18- to 21-year-olds access higher education, the total numbers are large and estimated to be around 23.3 million (GoI 2018).
2. As of July 2022, there are the following higher education institutions in India: state universities: 456; deemed to be universities: 126;

central universities: 54; and private universities: 419. See UGC (2022).

3. The National Knowledge Commission (NKC) was established in 2005, and was led by Sam Pitroda, known for initiating changes in the telecommunications domain. Far from being an open and democratic body that could have functioned through widespread consultations, the NKC has focused on promoting its own agenda and perspectives that endorse the opening up of the economy, being globally competitive, and developing the IT and Science and Technology disciplines over and above others.
4. For a definition and details of the 'edu-factory', see Federici and Caffentzis (2007).
5. Statement made by the Minister of State for Minority Affairs, saying that the government will establish four 'minority universities' with 50 per cent seats for religious minorities. See *The Hindu* (2012).
6. For more details on 'subjected personhood', see Vasavi (2006a).
7. For details see the website (http://www.igntu.ac.in/) of the IGNTU, Amarkantak.
8. For more details on the definition of 'vicinity', especially for social science research, see Vasavi (2011).
9. The 'Mandal agitation' or 'Anti-Mandal agitation' refers to the nationwide agitations by upper-caste students in 1990 against the extension of reservations to 'Other Backward Classes' or OBC students based on the recommendations of the Mandal Report, which had been submitted to the government in 1979, but which the then government sought to implement in 1990.
10. Du Bois referred to 'systemic miseducation' as formal education systems that did not enable the recognition of the rights of all people or integrated people into dominant ideas. He wrote this in the context of critiquing the poor quality of education that African-Americans received in the US at the turn of the twentieth century.
11. For a succinct summary of the Jesuits' educational work in India, see Joseph Satish (2012).
12. This is not a comprehensive review or assessment of CREST, and focuses only on identifying some of the orientation and approaches to STL that CREST has evolved. I would like to thank Professor D. D. Nampoothiri, the founding Director and current Director of CREST, for his support, and all the faculty and students who responded to the questionnaire I had sent them.

13. Cited from a response to a questionnaire mailed to CREST faculty.
14. CREST student response to a questionnaire.
15. Personal communication.
16. 'Place-based education' is a term now used commonly and associated with several alternative education groups. It refers to curricula which maybe designed keeping local contexts, and opportunities of the vicinity in mind.

APPENDIX I: PEDAGOGIES FOR STL

Key criteria that need to be achieved by STL programmes can include the following (rather than only achievement levels in academic performance or in grades):

- Confidence: Ability to speak up, represent self, and discuss issues;
- Body language: Eye contact, head and shoulder position, movement, postures, etc.;
- Comprehension: Ability to understand passages, summarise, and respond to questions, discussion and position on general issues;
- Critical thinking on key issues: Ability to assess social and cultural issues, prejudices and biases, popular practices, structures of power, etc.;
- Communication and decision-making abilities;
- Interpersonal skills, relating to peers, elders, persons in authority, and to subordinates;
- Knowledge of one's society and structures of power;
- Organisational capacity;
- Responsibility for the self and for the collective;
- Awareness of challenges at the local, regional, national, and global levels, and their interlinkages.

VII

NATIONAL EDUCATION POLICY 2020

Between Principles and Practice

Of the few education policy documents that the Government of India has produced, none has been as politically strategised and socially manipulative as the National Education Policy (henceforth NEP) 2020. While the draft, released immediately after the resounding victory of the BJP in the national elections for the second time in May 2019, is a copious 464 pages in length, the final version was approved in July 2020 amidst the Covid-19 situation and is a succinct document of sixty-five pages. The NEP committee, under the chairmanship of space scientist-administrator Dr K. Kasturirangan, consisted of a group of persons, most of whom seemed to have been selected not for their experience and standing in the field of education, but for their ideological orientation, which echoed that of the government.[1] Excluding many progressive groups and educationists from consultations, the NEP 2020 identifies four key goals for its vision of education for India: First, to realise the imperatives of 'sustainable development goals' (GoI 2020: 3); second, to draw on the 'rich heritage of ancient and eternal Indian knowledge and thought [which] has been a guiding light for this Policy' (ibid.: 4); third, to make India a 'global knowledge super power' (ibid.: 6); and fourth, it hopes to 'prepare India for the fourth industrial revolution' (ibid.: 37) and restore India's position as a 'Vishwa Guru' (ibid.: 39). The end result is a document that is mixed in its orientation. It draws on some progressive ideas, especially those related to early childhood and elementary education; endorses and builds on the aspirations of a burgeoning urban middle class; reinforces via a soft rhetoric the RSS-BJP's construction of the superiority of Indian traditions and knowledge systems; and projects a global ambition for India in the twenty-first century. Nearly two years since its promulgation, it would be appropriate to assess the key principles or ideas[2] that the NEP 2020 seeks to disseminate, and also factor in what new trends or practices it has initiated in the various domains of the education system. These will enable us to assess the significance the NEP 2020 will have for the education system in general, and examine its ability to address the differentiation and disjunction that mark the system.

Much of the content and orientation of the NEP 2020 is based on projecting an ambitious education policy without any significant and/or critical review or understanding of India's education system, its structural and processual characteristics, its limitations, and its impact on varied groups and classes. The NEP 2020 is largely an exercise in deploying a three-pronged approach to education reform. First, it seeks to implement structural changes that will facilitate centralisation and a command-and-control structure and process to education administration. Such foundational structural shifts, which are proposed to supposedly facilitate inclusion, efficiency and improved management, have significance for the political party/state's power over education. Second, the report's overall orientation towards education reflects that it endorses, upholds, and reinforces existing forms of social exclusion and cultural biases, thereby promoting a very limited and narrow perspective on education. Third, the NEP 2020 promotes the privatisation of education, especially higher and professional education, thereby challenging its own declared premises of facilitating education inclusion. At a broader political-economic level, such an approach will compromise the abilities of the state to uphold equality of access and quality of education.

The NEP 2020's positive and progressive points relate to four key issues. It places emphasis on early childhood care and education (ECCE) and recommends the extension of such centres called anganwadis and their facilities and support to tribal/Adivasi areas. It calls for a revival of the idea of 'school complexes', especially for rural areas, which the Kothari Commission[3] had promoted, and sees it as a way in which resources and personnel can be shared. Bucking popular demands and trends, it recommends mother tongue/home language as a medium of instruction up to Standard V. And, finally, the NEP 2020 elaborates several schemes and programmes to enhance teacher training and the professionalisation of teacher education, thereby challenging the widespread dismissal and long-entrenched neglect of teacher education. The report rightly challenges the rigid and punitive examination system and coaching culture, and calls for substantial reforms in the examination system, with subject options and increased number of opportunities for exam-taking.

Yet, what can be considered the positive or progressive elements of the report are rendered ineffective or marginal by several statements or suggestions that are contradictory to progressive ideas. While education in the mother tongue is asserted and promoted, the report also goes on to recommend mother-tongue education until Standard V, with only a rider that it can be continued up to Standard VIII (further discussed later in the chapter). This means that most schools, in the absence of a strict mandate to have mother-tongue education till Standard VIII, will opt to have English-medium education by default. Although the report asserts that it 'seeks to ensure inclusive and equitable quality education and promote lifelong learning opportunities for all by 2030' (GoI 2020: 3), it also advocates streaming children in classes as early as Standard VI into vocational education tracks, thereby overlooking the fact that tracking into vocational education at such an early age will only locate more disadvantaged children in non-professional tracks, and thereby deny them the opportunity to realise their own capabilities, or be educated into higher professions and life opportunities. What is perhaps the most glaring contradiction is the report's assertion to uphold '. . .traditional Indian values and all basic human and Constitutional values (such as *seva*, *ahimsa*, *swachchhata*, *satya*, *nishkam karma*, *shanti*, sacrifice, tolerance, diversity, pluralism, righteous conduct, gender sensitivity, . . .)' (ibid.: 16), even as it carefully avoids any reference to the importance of secular values, or to the centrality of secularism for a multi-religious democracy such as India.[4]

Restructuring the Education System

In the sweeping and foundational changes that it seeks to make, the NEP 2020 lays out a policy framework that has the potential to significantly restructure and reorient India's education system, but will largely retain the differentiated, hierarchical, and iniquitous structures and systems. Although education as a subject of administration is on the Concurrent List, the NEP report assumes it as a subject for the Centre and suggests sweeping organisational, administrative, and curricula changes at all levels, with little or no role for regional states. The report calls for redesignating the Ministry of Human Resource Development (MHRD) by its original name—the Ministry for Education—thereby returning the focus on education; this is a welcome move.

These new institutions recommended by the NEP 2019 (and excluded in the NEP 2020) include the establishment by an Act of Parliament of a new National Education Commission[5] (Rashtriya Shiksha Ayog [RSA]) to be chaired by the Prime Minister, and to be run by executive and advisory bodies, of which 50 per cent will consist of ministers and the other 50 per cent of educationists, academics, and civil society members. Several questions can be raised about the possibility (as mentioned in the draft but omitted in the final version) of such centralisation of the education system. What are the implications of having the Prime Minister chair the National Education Commission, which is to become the apex body for all education management and fund allocation? What are the criteria, standards, and processes by which members will be inducted into these new education governance institutions? These are not only key questions, but also concerns which must be raised, as they imply that the absorption of the education system into a political apparatus is imminent.

Under the super organisation of the Rashtriya Shiksha Ayog will be a range of new institutions such as:[6] the National Research Fund, National Higher Education Regulatory Authority (and State Education Regulatory Authorities in all states), Central Education Statistics Division (under NUEPA), National Repository of Educational Data, National Testing

Agency, Indian Institute of Translation and Interpretation, Multidisciplinary Education and Research Institutes or Indian Institutes of Liberal Arts, and General Education Council. Complementing these new organisational wings are schemes and programmes such as the National Scholarship Fund, Study in India Portal (for international students), and the Global Initiative for Academic Networks. Even as the establishment of these new institutions are listed, there is scant attention paid to reviewing the functioning of existing institutions. For example, the functioning of the National Assessment and Accreditation Council (NAAC) is not examined; instead, a series of new testing and monitoring institutions and agencies are suggested. The structural shifts suggested for higher education include the reorganisation of higher education institutes (HEI) into three types: (*i*) Research Universities; (*ii*) Teaching Universities; and (*iii*) Colleges. How such a restructuring will address the current problem of the divide between research and teaching (a practice that accounts for both poor pedagogic practices and inadequate research capacities at most educational institutes) is another issue that remains unaddressed. Assuring a substantial allocation of funds (to increase from the current average of less than 3 per cent of GDP to about 6 per cent by 2025), the report calls for a slew of institutions to be set up so as to enhance access to and the governance of education.

Such centralisation measures are visible at several levels. Overlooking the importance of decentralisation, the NEP 2020 fails to provide administrative measures for educational institutions such as the ashramshalas that cater to Adivasi regions and societies. The Ministry of Tribal Affairs (MoTA), that administers these institutions is not only placed as a low-ranked ministry, but has also not been assigned any special administrative capacity or additional funds to cater to the needs of the nearly 100 million citizens (specifically, at least the ten million who receive formal education) who fall under the rubric of Adivasis or tribals. Compare this to the fact that the IITs and IIMs (which cater to less than 1,00,000 students) have a special desk under the MHRD that supervises such institutions of 'excellence', or the fact that the Ministry of

Defence administers elite and exclusive schools that cater to the children of its officials.[7]

Differentiation and Disjunction

If the NEP 2020 is to be assessed in terms of its abilities/possibilities of addressing the twin problems of educational differentiation and disjunction, then the report falls short of any such orientation. In circumventing the possibility of a common school system that can ensure a genuine and full realisation of the Right to Education Act and ideals, the report seconds the continuity of a differentiated schooling system buttressed by an increasingly privatised higher education system. As Niranjanaradhya (2019) has pointed out in his overview of the NEP 2019, the Right to Education Act, which assures equal and quality education to all its citizens, has been disregarded. Such oversight or neglect is evident when one takes into account the several types of citizens. Although the report makes a case for inclusive education and mentions the need to cater to girls, Muslims, the urban poor, tribal, and transgender children, and for the establishment of educational institutions in underserved regions (including in areas which it identifies as 'aspirational districts'), the challenges of instituting equal and quality education for these disadvantaged groups is not spelled out.

Calling to position the higher education system on par with 'world-class' levels, the report makes the simplistic and deeply problematic (given the mass of educated unemployed and trends in new industrial and work systems) call to increase gross enrolment rates of higher education to 50 per cent of the population by 2035. Similarly, the NEP recommends the establishment of 'large multidisciplinary universities and colleges', with emphasis on 'online education, and Open Distance Learning (ODL)' (GoI 2020: 34), and endorses the expansion of mass higher education without any critical review of what poor-quality mass higher education has done to the youth, especially rural youth. Also overlooked is the existing problem of the large numbers of 'educated unemployed', who are themselves victims of the expansion of a mass and poor-quality higher education system.

Social Orientation

The report can be assessed for its stance vis-à-vis the principles of secularism, democracy, autonomy, merit/reservations, and for its ability to promote new knowledge systems and inclusive education systems. The NEP 2020 makes repeated assurances of 'autonomy' (mentioned twenty-one times) in education. Repeatedly, the report indicates that teacher autonomy, institutional, administrative, and curricula autonomy, including ensuring 'graded autonomy' (GoI: 34) for institutions will be fostered. Yet how will these be assured, both within educational institutions and by larger administrative structures? Recent incidents and trends, where scheduled speakers and seminars have been cancelled at the behest of vigilante groups,[8] indicate that neither the autonomy of administrative structures nor the agency of educationists is assured. Instead, what we are witness to is the extent to which it has become legitimate for those in power (both power which is formal, and that which is embedded in society) to question and curtail dissent in all forms (Deshpande 2016). Given these trends, the NEP 2020's silence on all these issues reinforces the fact that there are no guarantees of protection or assurance of an open intellectual environment. Failing to address this foundational challenge in India's educational system, the report loses the opportunity to realise a democratic society and polity. For unless there is both recognition and implementation of the importance and interlinks between 'education in democracy and democracy in education' (Gutman 1987), both education and democracy are bound to suffer.

Far from education being the source of the ability to question power, what we are witnessing is the ruling dispensation's ability to silence the right to question power. That this is what is intended is evident in the fact that although the draft report (NEP 2019) endorses the National Curriculum Framework (NCF) 2005 and its constructivist approaches, and recommends that it be devolved to the states by 2020, the government had, in 2021, formed a new committee to formulate a new National Curriculum Framework, again under the aegis of Dr K. Kasturirangan. Despite the NCF 2005's significant contribution in bringing together subject specialists across the various disciplines, who then contributed to the final NCF 2005, none of these stalwarts finds a place in the NCF 2021. Instead, in the new committee for NCF 2021, only members[9] who are close to the Sangh Parivar and to the current political dispensation, or whose contribution to education aligns closely to the religious nationalism being espoused, have found a place in the committee. Subsequently, what we observe is the extent to which efforts are being made to institute and disseminate a national curriculum that aligns more with '*desh bhakti*' or hyper-nationalism and fervid patriotism than one in which education can enable a discernment between knowledge and propaganda (Pathak 2021).

Calling for the 'interconnectedness of education', NEP 2020 identifies Liberal Arts Education (LAE) as education which combines art, music, language, orality, ethical and moral reasoning, constitutional values, socio-emotional learning, and health and safety. Yet, the NEP's own definition of 'liberal arts education' draws from the glory of 'ancient Indian knowledge systems' and cites the legacy of Banabhatta's *Kadambari* and its promotion of the '64 *Kalaas* or arts' as the foundation for legitimising and now promoting 'liberal arts' education in India (GoI 2020: 36). Such 'arts', the NEP 2020 identifies as including not only science and mathematics, but also 'singing and dancing' and the full panoply of technical sciences, as well as what are now called the 'soft skills' of communicative and social skills. Although it cites the classic universities of Nalanda, Takshashila, and other sites as part of India's lived knowledge systems, it does not indicate specific institutional structures, programmes, certification, and career paths that can lead to the retrieval and consolidation of these knowledge systems. But the key questions and challenges are to assess if and how the NEP 2020 will facilitate the realisation of a well-designed plan or a road map for LAE. How can such assertions for 'liberal education' be translated into actual pedagogical, textual, programmatic, and teaching-learning transactions? Current trends, especially since the passage of the NEP 2020, indicate the spread of 'illiberal' thinking, and as the case of Delhi University removing texts and writings by Dalit authors indicate, there is little intellectual, institutional, and state support for a wide range and bodies of knowledge. In addition, there are now instances of several new private universities, institutions, and even programmes being established that claim to be 'liberal arts', but which largely cater to the promotion of the new market-oriented disciplines of data science, logistics, and management. Further, the failure of the state to rein in vigilante groups who have asserted themselves in the contexts of seminars and lectures, faculty appointments, curricula and syllabi formation, etc., indicate that far from a 'liberal' environment, the NEP-based restructuring of education will only facilitate the loss of institutional autonomy, academic freedom, and creativity in education.

In its attempt to promote a diversity of knowledge systems and with an eye on endorsing an ancient India-centric perspective, the NEP 2020 draws on the idea of such knowledge[10] as '"Lok Vidya", i.e., important vocational knowledge developed in India, [which] will be made accessible to students through integration into vocational educational courses' (GoI 2020: 44). But the NEP 2020 limits the study of *lok vidya* or 'people's knowledge' to only vocational education, and neglects a spectrum of local and evolved knowledge systems and practices. Such knowledge systems, skills, and practices, which were tried and tested and which formed the bases of strategies of livelihood and identity, are now largely forgotten or unused, and are in a state of erosion. Can long-evolved bodies of knowledge and skills related to ecological conservation, agricultural practices, vernacular architecture, medicinal systems, metal smithy, weaving, arts and crafts, etc., all of which have significance not only as legitimate bodies of knowledge but also as foundations for alternative and new economies, be revamped to be part of vocational education, as well as of higher and professional education courses?

Although the NEP claims that the purpose of education is to achieve 'full human potential', develop an 'equitable and just society', and promote 'national development' (GoI 2020: 3), it fails to address the extant forms of indignity, humiliation, and erosion of personhood that the education system imposes on large numbers of learners. The fact that suicides by youth, especially by educated yet unemployed youth, has become one of the leading causes of unnatural death[11] should alert us to the severe limitations of India's mass higher education system. Disembedding rural societies and inadequate social support and opportunities among the working classes have resulted in the loss of their life-worlds and erosion of their local knowledge and skills, their sense of belonging, and in the general skills of liveability (such as resilience, managing scarcity, conflict negotiation, tolerance of cultural differences, and so on) (Vasavi 2020). As a greater number of youth are now targets of the expanding capitalist market and the deeply penetrating social media, they are more consumers and passive recipients of information than citizens or agents of their own life situations. Given such conditions and trends, it should be the responsibility of education policy makers to seek to provide education that would address such challenges and disadvantages.

In classifying all disadvantaged groups as 'underprivileged and socio-economically disadvantaged groups' (GoI 2020: 61), the NEP overlooks the need for appropriate and relevant educational programmes and institutions that can address generational disadvantages and the lack of social capital that many classes/castes bear. Although it is the BJP that has introduced 10 per cent reservations for upper castes in educational institutions, it makes no mention of the reservation system—the need to refine it, or, for better institutional processes, to realise the true spirit of caste-based reservations. The silence on the reservations issue is another indicator of the failure of the NEP 2020 to address one of the key disjunctions in India's higher education system. Yet, the silence itself is telling, inasmuch as it reflects the hostility that the BJP and its supportive networks and followers have against caste-based reservations in the education system, and their failure to understand the basic principles of restitutive justice. By ignoring the issue of caste-based reservations and asserting that there will be 'merit-based recruitments' (GoI 2020: 19), 'merit-based scholarships' (ibid.: 20), 'robust merit-based structure of tenure, promotion, and salary structure' (ibid.: 22), and also 'merit-based appointments of institutional leaders' (ibid.: 49), the NEP 2020 fails to recognise the advantages and larger social cultures that have enabled some people to be seen as, or to become, 'meritorious'. While one may consider the above phrases as statements that indicate the erasure of nepotism, biases, corruption, and illegal methods of educational institution-building, the NEP 2020's usage of 'merit' as an ideal and instrument is more akin to the simplistic notion that merit refers to inherent capacities, an idea which, as Sandel (2020) notes, overrides the social context and support system that enables such merit. In such a context, the negation and neglect of the caste-based reservation system and the widespread hostility against it indicate what upholding 'merit' has meant—that 'the meritocratic ideal is not a remedy for inequality; it is a justification of inequality' (ibid.: 122). In overlooking the need for a more nuanced and sensitive approach to enabling access to educational opportunities (Weisskopf 2004), and then scaffolding and nurturing different talents and capabilities, the NEP 2020 only flags the extent to which its commitment to liberal ideas of justice, equity, and social latitude—that is, allowing space and legitimacy for widely varied actors, positions, and views—is itself distanced from reality.

A superlative description of India's languages as 'the richest, most scientific, most beautiful, most expressive in the world' (GoI 2020: 14) leads to the NEP Commission recommending the study of India's languages and literatures as a way to foster unity and national integration. While the three-language formula has been qualified by a quick revision (post the protests in southern India when the draft report was released) to indicate the non-compulsion of Hindi, especially in the non-Hindi belts, the extent to which other Indian languages are to be promoted in the Hindi belts is not adequately elaborated. The NEP 2020 also fails to reckon with the problems that the spread of poor-quality English-medium education has created, and the need for a more clear-cut policy for languages and the medium of instruction. The problem of the education system having produced a large mass of 'educated youth' who are not capable of formal, written transactions in either their mother-tongues, regional languages, or in English[12] is not addressed by the report. This is the result of the spread of questionable 'English-medium schools', which have rendered learning into the rote production of English texts for examinations, but with inadequate written, spoken, and comprehension skills in both English and any other Indian language. If the NEP 2020 had recognised this issue, it could have built in the need for learning in the mother tongue at least up to middle school, and the need for a gradual introduction of English at the school level while also retaining competency in Indian languages. More specifically, it should have indicated what legal and administrative measures would be taken to curtail the spread of spurious English-medium schools, or provided enough of a boost to government schools to ensure that English competency becomes part of the state schooling system. Such stipulations could have ensured not only better language skills, and hence improved cognitive abilities, but the inclusion of the rich contemporary literature in Indian languages (for all courses, including professional education) could also enable learners to develop more nuanced and sensitive insights into the societies they come from. Instead, the incorporation and engagement of such literary works are missing at all levels, from high schools to professional education courses. While NEP 2020 endorses and legitimises a range of foreign/international languages to be taught, it has deliberately avoided the mention of Mandarin—an indication that the ongoing political tension with China has been extended to the domain of education, and a blinkered approach to the importance of one of the world's most important languages marks our National Education Policy.

Privatisation

As a key document that could and should have factored in the need for an appropriate balance between public and private players and interests in the domain of education, the NEP 2020 overall places emphasis on and promotes privatisation of education, especially at the level of higher education. Extending its predominantly neoliberal perspective to education, the NEP recommends the establishment of 'Special Education Zones', especially in 'aspirational districts', which it does not define or identify but which could refer to those areas or cities in which education enterprises can become the key sources of economy. Here, the report is upholding, without any critical review or understanding, institutions such as that of Rajasthan's Kota (and several others which are imitations of these), where training for entrance examinations to professional courses has become an industry, and whose real cost to parents and to the distortions that it generates in education are overlooked. Such distortions include not appreciating the real abilities and aptitudes of learners, neglecting the development of other knowledge and skill education systems, forcing the youth into a competitive mould that imposes enormous psychological and social stress, and levying huge financial burdens on parents, etc.

The oversight of such administrative measures extends to the failure of the NEP 2020 to suggest accountability, standards, and administrative supervision of private 'captive education institutions'. The spread of low fee-paying schools (Bose et al. 2021), especially those that claim to be English-medium, or those established by the more recent philanthro-capitalistic endeavours and those run by a range of spiritual/religious groups and institutions, all of whose quality of education and impact are questionable and have been problematic, receive no special attention. How are these to be administered and what norms would guide their functioning and rules of accessibility? The NEP 2020 not only fails to recognise or account for these trends and institutions, but by endorsing the legitimacy of such private players, it also seeks to justify the privatisation of education. The result is that instead of being seen and deployed as a 'public good', education is represented and related to as a private good, accessible to those with capital. Such privatisation leads not only to the commoditisation of education where profit-making takes precedence, but it also has implications for state-society relationships. As Cordelli elaborates in the context of critiquing the increasing 'privatisation of the state', it 'denies, to those subject to it, equal freedom, understood not as mere non-interference [of the state towards its people] but rather as a relationship of reciprocal independence [between the state and its people]' (2020: 9). The imbalance in the domain of education that a privatised state can create is evident in the extent to which private education players have created new forms of inequities in both access and context at all levels, and as can be seen in the field of medicine in India, they determine both the fees and charges for medical education and the criteria for admission and institutional cultures.

Drawing from its orientation towards promoting education for a technologically defined future and twenty-first century, the NEP promotes technical education in general and technology-based educational programmes, including online and distance education (ODL), in particular. While these may cater to the needs of some groups and persons, the NEP 2020 does not confront the fact that engaged learning needs to be more personal and an inter-subjective experience to offer a significant and meaningful education experience. In celebrating and promoting such technology-based mass learning, the NEP 2020 also neglects to factor in the extent to which online learning platforms have become a parallel education industry. Witness the growth of Byju's, an education service provider with billions of dollars of investment,[13] which has grown in presence and reach and made a mark at all levels of education. In failing to recognise such trends and their implications for education institution-building and quality, the NEP 2020 promotes an education market which will not enable the state to act as a regulatory body that can check on the quality and cost of education. In contrast to its celebration of technical education, the NEP 2020 neglects the importance of medical and healthcare knowledge and services, of which there is a severe deficit in the nation. Merely flagging the need for an exit examination at the end of the MBBS course does not address the fact that there need to be many more state-supported medical and ancillary healthcare education institutions. Similarly, agriculture education receives short shrift, indicating the lack of social imaginaries which recognise the key role that India's diverse agricultural systems can play, and the possibilities that lie in fostering new forms of rural-urban and agriculture-industry linkages. Here, the NEP has overlooked the fact that over the past two decades, the promotion of technical education (especially via private enterprises) has resulted in a glut in engineering colleges, while there are barely adequate numbers of agriculture education and training institutions.[14] The end results have manifested in several problems: while technical education institutions are faced with the challenges of dubious quality, poor academic endowments, and even closure,[15] the few agricultural courses available in the country are closely contested. Given the realities of extant and severe ecological degradation, the climate change emergencies, and the need for the nation to urgently restore its ecological foundations and cater to the economic, employment, and food needs of the nation, the NEP has been both indifferent and callous in failing to promote such agricultural, environmental, and conservation-oriented educational endeavours.

The overall orientation of the NEP 2020 indicates that it overlooks issues of democracy and secularism and the need for educational institutions to play a proactive role in addressing the inequities and injustices in society. In this, the NEP fails to set the foundation for making education a part of 'responsive institutions', which, as Acemoglu and Robinson (2013) describe in their seminal book, *Why Nations Fail*, are key to ensuring that nation-states enable the addressal of internal social wrongs and cater to the collective needs of citizens.

CONCLUSION

A final assessment of any education policy should be based on the scope it provides to the educational system and to educators to respond to conditions of emergency in the society and/or the nation. Recent trends indicate the extent to which the NEP 2020 is being deployed as an instrument and a medium for a larger political and hypernationalist agenda, rather than as a social governance mandate. That it fails to cater to the long-term and immediate needs of the society and nation has been evident in the failure of the education administration to respond to the education emergency that the Covid-19 lockdown and associated closures have compelled. As educational institutions opened in late 2021, after nearly eighteen months of closure, the education administration overlooked the immediate conditions, instead focusing on deploying the new NEP. As reports and studies have detailed, the prolonged closure of educational institutions and the inability of economically and regionally disadvantaged students to engage with online learning has led to an 'Education Emergency',[16] marked by 'learning loss' and high drop-out rates. The School Children's Online and Offline Learning (SCHOOL) survey, conducted in fifteen states and Union Territories with detailed interviews of 1,362 sample disadvantaged households, indicates that in rural areas, only 28 per cent of the children were studying regularly, while 37 per cent had discontinued studies and nearly half of the assessed children were unable to read more than a few words (Bakhla et al. 2021). Similarly, the continued delay and confusion associated with the conduct of NEET (National Eligibility cum Entrance Test) examinations since the onset of Covid-19 and the resulting disarray in the lives of students and the medical fraternity are examples of the lack of sensitivity and proactive orientation by the Ministry of Education. Despite these and other reports concerning the disarray and disruption caused by the prolonged closure of educational institutions, there has been little or no attention paid to addressing these issues. Instead, a 'business as usual' approach at all levels (from primary to higher and professional education) has been resorted to, thereby further damaging not only the educational experience of children and youth, but also failing to endow the management and teachers with the skills and capabilities to address such a situation.

On the chequered pathway that the NEP 2020 will follow, it is bound to forge many changes at the level of administrative structures, orientation, and access. Given the hubris with which it is being implemented and the shifts that are already emerging in India's educational landscape, the NEP 2020 will be the text that marks the life of most educationists and students. The contradictory vision that the NEP 2020 deploys in trying to forge an exclusionary and jingoistic nationalism, while also fitting the nation's large body of learners into the global economy, will be the key source of tension for the education system.In addition, the NEP committee members have largely overlooked the need to prepare the new generation of learners for a world that is increasingly characterised by complexity, uncertainty, and fragility (UNESCO 2021). While the manifestations of such challenging times are all too evident in our personal and national lives, the NEP 2020 has taken not only an ostrich approach, but also provides rosy and distorted guidelines that imagine India as a superpower (a Vishwa Guru), leading in the world of artificial intelligence, machine learning, and information technologies. In all of this, neither the teachers nor the learners are imagined as sensitive, engaged, and capable persons, but as minions subject to and produced by a rigid education system run on authoritarian lines. Such trends can be countered only if the NEP 2020 itself is short-lived, and alternatives—as either forms of resistance or as strategies for new, inclusive, and sensitive imaginaries for education—are made possible.

NOTES

1. Members of the NEP Committee were—Chair: Dr K. Kasturirangan (Former Chairman, ISRO [Indian Space Research Organisation]); Members: Vasudha Kamat (Former VC, SNDT Women's University, Mumbai); Manjul Bhargava (R. Brandon Fradd Professor of Mathematics, Princeton University); K. J. Alphonse (Former IAS officer who played a crucial role in achieving 100 per cent literacy rate in Kottayam and Ernakulam districts of Kerala); Ram Shankar Kureel (Former Founder VC, Baba Saheb Ambedkar University of Social Sciences, Madhya Pradesh); T. V. Kattimani (VC, Central Tribal University, Andhra Pradesh); Krishna Mohan Tripathy (Director of Education [Secondary] and Former Chairperson of Uttar Pradesh High School and Intermediate Examination Board); Mazhar Asif (Professor, Centre for Persian and Central Asian Studies, School of Language, Literature and Culture Studies, Jawaharlal Nehru University), and M. K. Sridhar (Former Member Secretary, Karnataka Knowledge Commission) (*Business Standard* 2017).
2. There have been several critical reviews of the NEP: for example, see Niranjanaradhya (2019); Gowda (2019); Hegde (2019), and Sadgopal (2011).
3. The Kothari Commission (1964–1966) had suggested the establishment of 'school complexes' where for every sub-region, a school complex would have not only up to the high school, but also teachers and resource facilities that could be shared across various schools.

4. See the essay by Chandan Gowda (2019) for a critical review of how the word and the idea of 'secularism' are missing in the NEP.
5. It is unclear as to why these institutions, including the overarching one, the RSA, are not mentioned in the final report. But the fact that this mega-structure (the RSA) and a range of other institutions were thought of and suggested is something that needs to be borne in mind.
6. Most of these new institutions are mentioned only in the draft NEP 2019, and the NEP 2020 mentions only a few of them. There is no note or rider as to whether the institutions and agencies mentioned in the draft will be implemented or not.
7. The Lawrence, Lovedale (Tamil Nadu) and the Lawrence, Sonawar (Himachal Pradesh) schools have representatives from the Department of Defence on their governing bodies, and the property or land on which they are situated are considered properties of the state.
8. Over the years, several vigilante groups have enforced the cancellation of seminars and appointments in various universities. These include incidents at Banaras Hindu University (BHU), Ahmedabad University, Delhi University, and others. For details on the case in Madhya Pradesh, see, *Scroll.in* (2021).
9. Members of the committee for National Curriculum Framework, 2021 include the following: Dr K. Kasturirangan (an astrophysicist and space administrator); Govind Prasad Sharma (Head of Vidya Bharati, a unit of the RSS); Michael Danino (author of the book, *The Lost River: On the Trail of the Saraswathi* and supporter of theories of Aryan culture); M. K. Shridhar (former national president of ABVP and secretary of Bengaluru's RSS unit); T. C. Kattimani (VC of the Central Tribal University, Andhra Pradesh); Milind Kamble (a Dalit entrepreneur who was nominated to the IIM at Jammu); Jagbir Singh (RSS representative and Member of Haryana's school education committee); Dhir Jhingran (Former IAS officer, and founder member of Language and Learning Foundation); Mahesh Chandra Pant (Present Chancellor of the NIEPA); Najma Akhtar (VC, Jamia Millia Islamia University); Manjul Bhargava (Fields Medal-winning American mathematician of Indian origin); Shankar Maruwada (Co-founder and CEO, EkStep Foundation who has worked on large scale projects such as the AADHAAR). See https://pib.gov.in/PressReleaseIframePage.aspx?PRID=1756800 (accessed June 2022).

10. The idea of 'lok vidya' or 'people's knowledge' was elaborated by the Lok Vidya Jan Andolan group, which has been working on alternative learning and education practices since 2011.
11. See the National Crime Records Bureau (NCRB 2020) reports on suicides among youth.
12. For more details, see some of the learning assessment reports by the Annual Status of Education Reports (ASER).
13. Byju's is an online learning app and system that caters to elementary through professional (medicine, engineering) education. Currently valued at US$ 11 billion, the education portal and app has gained a tremendous number of enrolments since the Covid-19 lockdown (*Livemint* 2020).
14. In the academic year 2020–2021, there were 8,985 engineering colleges and only 134 government agricultural colleges or universities and ten private agricultural institutions (source: ICAR and MHRD data).
15. Several engineering colleges in Tamil Nadu, Andhra Pradesh, and Karnataka have been closed for lack of adequate enrolments.
16. See the *Frontline* 2021 special issue, 'Education Emergency', 38(20).

VIII

EPILOGUE

Reimagining Education

For long years now, we have lamented the crises of our education system—its divorce from larger society, its creation of unemployable persons, its questionable orientation, its poor functioning, and the continued exclusion of the poor and the disadvantaged. Much of the narrative of the crises has become commonsensical, although thorough research on each of the themes is awaited. But we now need to reimagine what direction and orientation our education system must take, for we are at a juncture where, alongside great and widespread expectations of mass elementary education, there is near and complete despondency and demoralisation about the state of education itself. Between these poles of hope and despair, we must cast our eyes on the immediate and the distant goals and means, and reimagine educational ideas and practices which will enhance individual capacities and collective responsibilities, foster the building of a democratic society and nation, infuse moral strength and critical thinking—in short, challenge the reproduction of an iniquitous and hierarchical society. There is an urgent need to do so as education today is being imagined and directed by a range of players for whom education works primarily to serve their own goals and purposes. First are the education entrepreneurs who, in the context of neoliberalism, are being aided and abetted by the state, and who see the education sector as an investment-worthy site. They run educational institutions as profit-making enterprises in which the language of the market predominates. Their functioning is along the lines of manufacturing companies, in which managerialism and its norms and idioms of profit, control, competitiveness, productivity, and market values prevail over the philosophy of education as a public good.

In the current climate, with the growing dominance of the market, we are witnessing the submission of the education agenda to the norms of the market, to the extent that there are now calls for a 'just-in-time education' to match the 'just-in-time management' practices and industrial production systems. Forsaken here are the very requirements of the basics of education for a life and not merely a livelihood. Closely aligned to such calls are the advocates of high technology, who assume that the problems of accessibility, mass outreach, and the urgency of bridging the education gap can be met by the wonders of technology. The recent success and visibility of the information technology industries and the iconisation of the computer has only enhanced this cacophony, and IT education and 'IT-based learning' are advanced as a magic wand that can address the problems of accessibility, and be the route through which the potential of the nation to become a world superpower can be realised. So popular have the IT industries become that they now define the higher education options for a large proportion of adolescents, who seek careers in the industry irrespective of their aptitude or interest in the subject. Drawn by this new global imaginary and ambition are a range of international development and aid agencies, who aim to direct India's education towards producing the globally viable worker, whose efficiency and universally valid cognitive skills must be assessed through standard tests, reviews, and retraining.

In many ways, equally insidious are the cultural and religious fundamentalists who see in education the opportunity to foster sectarian agendas that have both political and cultural purposes. The growth of such establishments has been prolific, with Saraswati Mandirs[1] sprouting in even remote areas and madrassas emerging as alternative learning spaces for Muslims. New-age and charisma-based religious movements now see education as the foundation on which to build their new devotee-clients. A testimony to this is evident in the chains of schools and higher education institutions run by organisations that are gaining presence, such as the Mata Amritanandamayi group, Isha Foundation, Sri Sri Ravi Shankar Foundation, and others. What such education, fostered on ideas of religious indoctrination, supremacy, and the construction of religious 'others', will imply for the social fabric of the nation are issues that remain unaddressed. An unexpected section that remains resistant to reimagining education is the established education apparatus—the range of organisations and institutions that supposedly oversee the 'development' of education, but are entrenched in either outdated or borrowed notions of education, or mired in bureaucratic tangles which render them largely dysfunctional. Oblivious to the realities, needs, and aspirations of people, these institutions have continued to produce and reproduce educational paraphernalia that is largely irrelevant and de-contextualised. This may explain the focus on textbooks, the exam orientation, and the resistance of our education system to the idea that education can be a creative and critical exercise.

For education to be reclaimed and reimagined as a key tenet of our lives, as we live it now and for what it can be tomorrow, we must pose some key questions. These are: What type of education can/must we have? Is it adequate to have literacy for the masses but a global education for the elite? Much of India's history of education indicates this parallel trajectory—poor quality education for the masses and islands of excellence for the elite. That such a differentiated system will only reproduce the inequities of society, and therefore challenge the very idea of the nation being a democracy, is an issue that continues to be overlooked. The language divide, with English for the elite and the vernacular languages for the masses, impedes any attempt to bring about a conversation among different socio-economic classes. For many of us, schooled in the language and thought of English, our inability to engage with the Hindi and regional language speakers and the body of knowledge in these languages is not only our handicap, but also a great in-built divide that stymies any creative collaboration. Recognising the strength of our plural and diverse language pool requires a rethinking of the language policy, so that the current refrain of the inevitability of English in the context of globalisation, which has led to the erosion of polyglot traditions, can be halted.

To this must be added the urgency of ensuring that goals and means are adopted so that accessibility can be assured and education becomes the fount of a new society. How a democratic society and nation can ensure universal access to types of learning that will ensure an organic continuity of their liveable skills and knowledge, a celebration of their positive heritage, and also facilitate their engagement with a larger world remains a challenge. What interlinkages must there be between the state, the society, and the market so as to deliver an education system that recognises the changing nature and relationship between these three? The interlinkages between the three are often noted and accepted as inevitable. Yet, today there are unprecedented and sharp shifts in society, making its very structures nebulous, and marking the lives of a majority by precarity and uncertainty. Macro- and micro-economic, socio-cultural and political processes are disembedding and re-embedding our societies. Agricultural societies are subject to a sharp erosion of their knowledge base, know-how, and skills. Artisans, handicraft workers, and a range of occupations and skills related to medicine, metallurgy, carpentry, and architecture, among others, which were based on inherited and orally transmitted knowledge systems, have been either made redundant or marginalised as inappropriate for a modern economy. In this context, what requirements of society must education cater to? Should the ancestral knowledge base be privileged over the drive towards the market-determined service and industrial economies? Or is a combination of both possible, where ancestral skills and knowledge can be meshed with new technology and know-how? In seeking to integrate such issues, it may be critical for our curriculum designers to rethink the curricula and move from privileging teaching to privileging learning, so that both teachers and students see learning as a continuous, open, and dialogic process.

The role of the state in matters of education must be interrogated, in particular the tendency to proclaim policies without attention to their implementation and impact. Take, for example, the reservation policy—lost in a populist posturing that provides no supportive programmes for disadvantaged students—which has served to heighten hostility between caste groups, even as the benefits themselves remain questionable. Urgent reviews of the policy, its functioning, and impact are required if the historical disadvantages of select communities are to be addressed through positive discrimination. Attention must be paid to the processes of selection and development of tailored programmes, adequate academic and social support, and periodic review of the policy itself. It is important that the attempt to provide an advantage to historically disadvantaged communities does not merely become a populist political game with negative consequences for the actual programme.

The nature of different regions and their economies and societies compounds the difficulty in pursuing singular education agendas. Neoliberal states, in subscribing to the agenda of the market and privileging the market, overlook the rights of a large number to access education. But even radical, left-leaning states subscribe to populist demands, and in privileging access and numbers overlook the need for quality in education. Within this context of altering societal structures and ineffective state support, the market has come to define the markers of success. Ideas of excellence in education are now determined by the pay packet that students, primarily from the techno-managerial schools, can command, while little encouragement is provided for a range of other subjects and knowledge.

What institutional design must we consider so that institutions function according to democratic norms, where interdisciplinary engagements are made possible, and the separation of research and teaching is bridged? Although citing the limitation of funds has become a refrain, a closer look would reveal that more than the availability of funds, it is the entrenched democracy deficit that acts as the single most important reason for institutional malfunction. Most institutions of learning exhibit a contradiction in their functioning. In the textual and formal context, they are to be rule-based institutions. Yet, in most cases, the writ of the head of the organisation runs large, and a single individual is able to make or break an institution. Students then carry with them the culture of autocracy, an absence of norms of transparency and accountability, and reproduce in their personal and collective lives the culture of their *alma mater*. No surprise, then, that the assertions of violence in the public life of the nation come not from the non-literate, but from those who are lettered and products of varied educational institutions. Periodic social auditing of institutions that makes democratic functioning the hallmark of their performance must be instituted, so that transparency of decision-making and accountability are ensured. Recognising not only the agency of teachers (for example, hitherto often teachers are not part of management and decision-making bodies) but also their democratic rights and abilities to realise their own potential will be key to facilitating a major change in the education system.

Which intellectual traditions must we subscribe to? Or, what new intellectual orientation must be generated by the new institutions? The vestiges colonialism left in its wake continue to influence our institutions and processes, and indigenous or even hybrid or newly-evolved forms of intellectual traditions are hard to come by. Recent attempts to 'Indianise' the curricula or lend it specific cultural dimensions have only sought narrow and poorly developed content, without any serious or appropriate educational modules being developed. Further, can the disciplinary divides be challenged so as to generate new interdisciplinary practices in which knowledge becomes holistic and competency in a range of disciplines is recognised? The sharply dichotomised 'two cultures' of the natural sciences versus the humanities and social sciences must be bridged in the learning paradigms so that composite schools that relate to the complex realities of the physical and social world can be developed. What role should educators play in the life of education institutions, students, society, and the state? There is an urgency to create a sense of belonging to institutions among educators, so that education institution-building can be enhanced. This is central, as over the years the agency of teachers/educators has been eroded, making them insecure, isolated, and insular individuals, submissive to structures that determine their employment. The growing distance between teachers and students, in which the relationship does not go beyond the formal and predominantly textbook-based teaching, needs to be addressed. How can the teacher-student relationship foster collaborative endeavours and make for the growth of both?

The absence of a strong and independent community of scholars and educators has led to the co-option of some by the state. Scholars either blindly endorse the policies or programmes of the state or, as in more recent years of neoliberalism, join international aid agencies to become part of their local data collection teams without providing any independent intellectual inputs. This subordination and nexus must be challenged to assert the independent and autonomous nature of intellectuals, and enable them to stand for ideas that go beyond the demands of political and/or personal economic interests. Equally, the submission of educators to the market must be challenged so that high compensation does not become a criterion for engaging with or producing information that is of limited value and use.

Just as the orientation, agency, and linkages of educators and intellectuals need to be reviewed and their independence and autonomy asserted, similar attention must be paid to the impress of education on the life of youth. Given the discourse of the expanding global economy marked by flexible capital and the need for flexible skills, should our youth, one of the most numerous in the world, be subject to these norms and be trained for careers that enable them to be flexible workers? Or should education be the foundation on which youth can become active citizens and also productive workers? Given that for a majority of our youth, high schools and colleges either mark them as unfit for work or alienate them from their families and communities, the challenge of imparting an education that can endorse the pluralistic identities of youth and forge a collective identity of shared citizenship remains.

Finally, how can we retain the plurality of our education system even as we question the growing differentiation of education institutions and programmes? Even as the variety of educational institutions with their historical roots in regional cultures and religions is fast diminishing, a new range of education institutes is taking root. As private edu-enterprises gain a foothold, how these would cater to the needs of students and address the idea of education, of fostering a common weal, are issues that remain unaddressed. While the growing differentiation of schools reflects the heightened differentiation in society, there is a need to consider the design and implementation of a common school system that can address the current problem of education reproducing the social and economic differences and divides in the nation. Amid these claims and assertions, there has been a silencing of academic voices and those of others who have engaged with education, its practice, and its institution-building. Academics and civil society members must reclaim the agendas of and for education so as to make it an inclusive and pluralistic enterprise that caters to individual capabilities and enables collective responsibilities.

All these questions require that we rethink and reimagine education so that the strength of our pluralistic traditions is retained while enabling learning for new lives and livelihoods. From the enabling of mass basic but high-quality education to the feasibility of specialisations in higher education, we need to balance the demands of diversity with those for regulation. This is crucial, lest we submit and subordinate ourselves to the markings of the new regimes of education, in which either subscription to simplified and distorted histories or cultural orientations, or formats of testing and certification become punitive compulsions on students. Far from the promise of building on the knowledge and skills of people and enabling every child to learn from their environment and from the outside world, there is currently a hegemonic model that seeks to produce a globally adaptable worker. It is this reduction by the new education regime of every student into merely a worker in a global economy, or a member who will bear the identities of constructed religious nationalism, that we must vehemently protest.

In contrast to the gut-wrenching scenarios with which I introduced this book and its themes, I think we must imagine new scenarios in which a range of positive trends can be achieved. These include the establishment of common schools that are of equal quality and standards, of learning transactions that make education a truly joyful experience, of enabling education institutions to become responsive institutions that cater to the emotional, social, and intellectual needs of all learners, and where teachers are themselves continuous learners. In any reimagining of education, we must seek to realise the individual potential of every learner who can also contribute to the collective well-being of society, as well as the need to prepare them for a world marked not only by precarity and uncertainty, but also one in which all received ideas can be challenged and new paradigms, parameters, and performance markers can be made possible.

NOTE

1. Saraswati Mandirs are pre-schools and schools, which are being established across the country by organisations affiliated directly to the RSS, or by various Hindu outfits, that seek to disseminate Hindu cultural values in education.

BIBLIOGRAPHY

Acemoglu, Daron and James A. Robinson. 2013. *Why Nations Fail: The Origins of Power, Prosperity and Poverty.* Noida: Hachette India.

Acharya, Paromesh. 2002. 'Education: Panchayat and Decentralisation. Myths and Reality'. *Economic and Political Weekly* 38(8).

Agamben, Giorgio. 2007. *The Coming Community,* Michael Hardt (trans.). Minneapolis: University of Minnesota Press.

Agarwal, Arun. 1999. 'Community in Conservation: Tracing the Outlines of an Enchanting Concept'. In Roger Jeffery and Nandini Sundar (eds), *A New Moral Economy for India's Forestry? Discourses of Community and Participation.* New Delhi: Sage.

Ambedkar, B. R. 1945 [1936]. *Annihilation of Caste* (*With a Reply to Mahatma Gandhi*). Mumbai: Government of Maharashtra Press.

———. 1987 [1936]. *Annihilation of Caste.* Bangalore: Dalit Sahitya Akademy.

Amatullah, Shaima. 2022. 'Contesting the Secular School: Everyday Nationalism and Negotiations of Muslim Childhoods'. *Children's Geographies.* Available at DOI: 10.1080/14733285.2022.2059342 (accessed June 2022).

Anita, B. K. 2000. *Village, Caste and Education.* Jaipur: Rawat Publications.

Anveshi. 2002. 'Caste and the Metropolitan University'. *Economic and Political Weekly* 37(12).

Anyon, Jean. 2006. 'Social Class, School Knowledge and the Hidden Curriculum'. In Lois Weis, Cameron McCarthy and Greg Dimitriadis (eds), *Ideology, Curriculum, and the New Sociology of Education: Revisiting the Work of Michael Apple.* London: Routledge.

Apple, Michael and Nancy King. 1985. 'Economics and Control in Everyday School Life'. In S. Shukla and Krishna Kumar (eds), *Sociological Perspectives in Education: A Reader.* New Delhi: Chanakya Publications.

Apple, Michael. 1993. *Official Knowledge: Democratic Education in a Conservative Age.* New York: Routledge.

Archer, Margaret. 1982. 'Introduction: Theorising About the Expansion of Educational Systems'. In Margaret Archer (ed.), *The Sociology of Educational Expansion: Take-Off, Growth and Inflation in Educational Systems.* London: Sage.

Arnot, Madeleine. 2006. 'Retrieving the Ideological Past: Critical Sociology, Gender Theory, and the School Curriculum'. In Lois Weis, Cameron McCarthy and Greg Dimitriadis (eds), *Ideology, Curriculum, and the New Sociology of Education: Revisiting the Work of Michael Apple.* London: Routledge.

Arunima, G. 2017. 'Thought, Policies, and Politics: How May We Imagine the Public University in India?' *Kronos: Southern African Histories,* November.

ASER Centre. 2014. *Annual School Education Report.* Mumbai: Pratham.

ASER. 2017. *Annual Status of Education Report 2017.* Mumbai: Pratam.

Bakhla, Nirali et al. 2021. 'Locked Out: Emergency Report on School Education'. *Frontline* 38(20): 8–18. Also available at https://frontline.thehindu.com/cover-story/locked-out-emergency-report-on-school-education-school-survey-2021/article36549535.ece (accessed June 2022).

Balagopalan, Sarada and Ramya Subramanian. 2003. 'Dalit and Adivasi Children in School: Some Preliminary Research Themes and Findings'. *IDS Bulletin, Special Issue on Education Inclusion and Exclusion: Indian and South African Perspectives* 34(1).

Balakrishnan, Pulapre. 2010. *Economic Growth in India: History and Prospect.* New Delhi: Oxford University Press.

Banerji, Rukmini. 1997. 'Why Don't Children Complete Primary School? A Case Study of a Low-Income Neighbourhood in Delhi'. *Economic and Political Weekly* 32(32).

———. 2000. 'Poverty and Primary Schooling: Field Studies from Mumbai and Delhi'. *Economic and Political Weekly* 35(10).

Banerjee, Abhijit, Rukmini Banerji, Esther Duflo, Rachel Glennerster, Daniel Kenniston, Stuti Khemani, and Marc Shotland. 2007. 'Can Information Campaigns Raise Awareness and Local Participation in Primary Education?' *Economic and Political Weekly* 42(15) 1365–1372.

Bardhan, Pranab. 1984. *The Political Economy of Development in India,* Expanded edition. New Delhi: Oxford University Press.

Batra, Poonam. 2009. 'Teacher Empowerment: The Education Entitlement-Social Transformation Traverse'. *Contemporary Education Dialogue* 6(2).

Bauman, Z. 2004. *Wasted Lives: Modernity and Its Outcasts.* Cambridge: Polity Press.

Benei, Veronique. 2008. *Schooling India: Hindus, Muslims and the Forging of Citizens.* New Delhi: Permanent Black.

Benhabib, Seyla. 1992. *Situating the Self: Gender, Community and Postmodernism in Contemporary Ethics.* London: Polity Press.

Bhattacharya, Dwaipayan. 2001. 'Civic Community and Its Margins: School Teachers in Rural West Bengal', *Economic and Political Weekly* 36(8).

Biesta, Gert and Anders Safstrom. 2018. 'A Manifesto for Education'. *Praxis Educativa* 22(2): May–August. Available at http://dx.doi.org/10.19137/praxiseducativa-2018-220203 (accessed June 2022).

Bögenhold, D. 2001. 'Social Inequality and the Sociology of Life Style: Material and Cultural Aspects of Social Stratification'. *American Journal of Economics and Sociology* 60(4).

Bolay, Mathhieu and Jeanne Rey. 2021. 'Frontiers of Cosmopolitanism: Educational Enclaves and the Extractive Roots of International Schools'. *Critique of Anthropology* 41(4): 421–437.

Booth, A. and A. Crouter. 2001. *Does it take a Village? Community Effects on Children, Adolescents and Families.* Sussex: Psychology Press.

Bourdieu, Pierre. 2010. 'Education and Domination'. In P. Bourdieu, *Political Interventions: Social Science and Political Action, Collected Essays of Pierre Bourdieu.* New Delhi: Navayana.

Bourdieu, P. and L. Boltanski. 1978. 'Changes in Social Structure and Changes in the Demand for Education'. In Stephen J. Ball (ed.), *Sociology of Education: Major Themes, Vol. I: Theories and Methods.* London: Routledge.

Bourdieu, Pierre and Loic Wacquant. 1992. *An Invitation to Reflexive Sociology.* Chicago: University of Chicago Press.

Bose, Sukanya, Priyanta Ghosh, Arvind Sardana and Manohar Boda. 2021. 'Regulation and Informal Market for Schools in Delhi', Working Paper No. 340. New Delhi: National Institute of Public Finance and Policy.

Bowles, Samuel and Herbert Gintis. 1976. *Schooling in Capitalist America.* London: Routledge and Kegan Paul.

Bruner, Jerome. 1996. *The Culture of Education.* Cambridge, Massachusetts.: Harvard University Press.

Business Standard. 2017. '9-member panel to prepare final draft of National Education Policy', 26 June. Available at https://www.business-standard.com/article/news-ians/9-member-panel-to-prepare-final-draft-of-national-education-policy-117062600537_1.html (accessed June 2022).

CABE. 1993. 'CABE Committee on Decentralised Management of Education', Report. New Delhi: Dept. of Education, Ministry of Human Resource Development, GoI. Available at http://14.139.60.153/bitstream/123456789/217/1/Report-CABE%20Committee%20on%20Decentralised%20Management%20of%20Education_D07782.pdf (accessed August 2022).

Caffentzis, George, 2008. 'A Critique of Commodified Education and Knowledge (From Africa to Maine)', A Russell Scholar Lecture, 12 February. University of Southern Maine. Available at https://thecommoner.org/wp-content/uploads/2020/06/caffentzis_critiqueeducation.pdf (accessed June 2022).

Calhoun, Craig. 1991. 'Indirect Relationships and Imagined Communities: Large-Scale Social Integration and the Transformation of Everyday Life'. In Pierre Bourdieu and James Coleman (eds), *Social Theory for a Changing Society.* Boulder: Westview.

Chandhoke, Neera. 2003. 'A Critique of the Notion of Civil Society as the "Third Sphere"'. In Rajesh Tandon and Ranjita Mohanty (eds), *Does Civil Society Matter? Governance in Contemporary India.* New Delhi: Sage.

Chowdhry, P. 2010. *Contentious Marriages, Eloping Couples: Gender, Caste, and Patriarchy in Northern India.* New York: Oxford University Press.

Clarke, Prema. 2001. *Teaching and Learning: The Culture of Pedagogy.* New Delhi: Sage Publications.

Cohen, Anthony, 1985. *The Symbolic Construction of Community.* London: Routledge.

Cordelli, Chiara. 2020. *The Privatized State.* New Jersey: Princeton University Press.

Counts, George S. 1996 [1932]. *Dare Schools Build a New Social Order?* New York: John Day Company.

Cranton, Patricia. 2006. 'Fostering authentic relationships in the transformative classroom'. *New Directions for Adult and Continuous Education* 109.

Daswani, C. J., N. V. Varghese, and R. Govinda. 1997. *Primary Education in India – A Status Report, Vol. I: Citizens' Initiative for Primary Education in India.* Bangalore: Navbharat Press.

Deccan Herald. 2011. 'KPSC ex-chief held', 8 October. Available at https://www.deccanherald.com/content/196211/kpsc-ex-chief-held.html (accessed June 2022).

Deshpande, Satish. 2011. 'Social Justice and Higher Education in India Today: Markets, States, Ideologies and Inequalities in a Fluid Context'. In M. Nussbaum and Z. Hasan (eds), *Equalising Access: Affirmative Action in Higher Education in India, United States and South Africa*. New Delhi: Oxford University Press.

——— (ed.). 2014. *The Problem of Caste*. New Delhi: Sage.

———. 2016. 'The Public University after Rohith-Kanhaiya'. *Economic and Political Weekly* 51(11).

Dev, M. and M. Venkatanarayana. 2011. 'Youth Employment and Unemployment in India', Working Paper 2011–009. Mumbai: Indira Gandhi Institute of Development Research.

Devy, Ganesh. 2017. *The Crisis Within: On Knowledge and Education in India*. New Delhi: Aleph Book Company.

Dewey, John. 1916. *Democracy and Education*. New York: McMillan.

———. 1920. *The School and Society*. Chicago: Chicago University Press.

Dyer, Caroline. 1996. 'Primary Teachers and Policy Innovation in India: Some Neglected Issues'. *International Journal of Educational Development* 16(1).

Education World. 2007. 'Faltering High-Potential Initiative', September. Available at https://www.educationworld.in/faltering-high-potential-initiative/ (accessed June 2022).

———. 2021. 'Karnataka: Government teachers threaten protest over new recruitment rules', 15 December. Available at https://www.educationworld.in/karnataka-government-teachers-threaten-protest-over-new-recruitment-rules/ (accessed June 2022).

Educational Initiatives and WATIS. n. d. 'Quality Education Study: Student Learning Outcomes', EI Working Paper Series, Issue 14. Bengaluru: Wipro Applying Thought in School. Available at https://www.ei.study/newEIWebsite/eiasset/pdf/wp-14-qes2.pdf (accessed August 2022).

Faust, David and Richa Nagar. 2001. 'Politics of Development in Postcolonial India: English Medium Education and Social Fracturing'. *Economic and Political Weekly* 36(30).

Federici, Silvia and George Caffentzis. 2007. 'Notes on the Edu-Factory and Cognitive Capitalism'. *The Commoner* 12. Available at https://thecommoner.org/wp-content/uploads/2020/06/Federici-Caffentzis-Notes-of-the-edu-factory-and-cognitive-capitalism.pdf (accessed June 2022).

Fernandes, Leela and Patrick Heller. 2006. 'Hegemonic Aspirations'. *Critical Asian Studies* 38(4).

Florestal, Ketleen and Robb Cooper. 1997. *Decentralisation of Education: Legal Issues*. Washington D.C.: World Bank.

Fraser, N. 1997. 'From Redistribution to Recognition? Dilemmas of Justice in a Postsocialist Age'. In N. Fraser, *Justice Interruptus: Critical Reflections on the 'Postsocialist' Condition*. New York: Routledge.

Freire, Paulo. 1999. 'Education and Community Involvement'. In M. Castells et al. (eds), *Critical Education in the New Information Age*. London: Rowman and Littlefield.

Fricker, Miranda. 2011. 'Powerlessness and Social Interpretation'. In D. Steel and F. Gualla (eds), *The Philosophy of Social Sciences Reader*. London: Routledge.

Frontline. 2022. 'Hijab verdict: Lifting the veil on essentiality', 22 April. Available at https://frontline.thehindu.com/social-issues/karnataka-hijab-verdict-lifting-the-veil-on-essentiality/article38468622.ece (accessed June 2022).

Gardner, John W. 1996. 'School and Community'. *Community Education Journal* 23(6–8).

Gilding, Paul. 2011. *The Great Disruption: How the Climate Crisis Will Transform the Global Economy*. London: Bloomsbury Publishing.

Giroux, Henri. 1999. 'Rethinking Cultural Politics and Radical Pedagogies in the Work of Antonio Gramsci'. *Educational Theory* 49(1).

Gorder, Chris Van. 2008. 'Paulo Friere's Pedagogy for the Children of the Oppressors: Educating for Social Justice among the World's Privileged.' *Journal of Pedagogy, Pluralism, and Practice* 4(1).

Government of India (GoI). 1966. *Education and National Development: Report of the Education Commission*. New Delhi: Ministry of Education.

———. 1996. *Restructuring of Elementary, Primary and Non-Formal Education in the Context of the New Panchayat Raj,* Commission Papers. New Delhi: Ministry of Human Resource Development.

———. 1998. *DPEP Moves on: Towards Universalising Basic Education.* New Delhi: Ministry of Human Resource Development.

Government of India (GoI) 2014. *Census of India: Provisional Population Data*. Available at www: censusindia.gov.in (accessed June 2022).

———. 2018. *Educational Statistics at a Glance.* New Delhi: Ministry of Human Resources Development.

———. 2019. National Education Policy 2019. New Delhi: Ministry of Human Resource and Development. Available at https://www.education.gov.in/sites/upload_files/mhrd/files/Draft_NEP_2019_EN_Revised.pdf (accessed May 2022).

———. 2020. National Education Policy 2020. New Delhi: Ministry of Human Resource and Development. Available at https://www.education.gov.in/sites/upload_files/mhrd/files/NEP_Final_English_0.pdf (accessed June 2022).

Govinda, R. and Rashmi Diwan (eds). 2003. *Community Participation and Empowerment in Primary Education.* New Delhi: Sage.

Govinda, R. (ed.). 2011. *Who Goes to School? Exploring Exclusion in Indian Education.* New Delhi: Oxford University Press.

Gowda, Chandan. 2019. 'Narrowing Down Education', *Bangalore Mirror,* 04 June. Available at https://bangaloremirror.indiatimes.com/opinion/views/narrowing-down-education/articleshow/69639378.cms (accessed June 2022).

Gujar, Bhoju Ram and Ann Gold. 2005. 'Messenger between the Worlds: A Village Headmaster's Global Orientations', Manuscript draft of a presentation for a conference on 'Children, Youth, and their Education in a Globalising India', 22–24 December. Varanasi: Centre for Postcolonial Education.

Gutman, Amy. 1987. *Democratic Education.* Princeton, N.J: Princeton University Press.

———. 1990. 'Democratic Education in Difficult Times'. *Teachers' College Record* 92(1).

Hegde, Sasheej. 2019. 'Education on Education – Reclamation, and Other Mediations'. *Kafila,* 24 September. Available at https://kafila.online/2019/09/24/education-on-education-reclamation-and-other-mediations-sasheej-hegde/ (accessed June 2022).

Herring, Ronald and Rina Agarwala. 2006. 'Restoring Agency to Class: Puzzles for the subcontinent'. *Critical Asian Studies* 38(4).

Hindustan Times. 2016. 'Delhi to Ranchi: Protests over Dalit suicide turn into national movement', 27 January. Available at https://www.hindustantimes.com/india/dalit-scholar-suicide-protests-turn-into-movement-against-caste-bias/story-hRWDjL0qedC7pj49B5JM7M.html (accessed June 2022).

Hindustan Times. 2017. 'Delhi's Ramjas College cancels invite to JNU students Umar Khalid, Shehla Rashid', 8 March. Available at https://www.hindustantimes.com/delhi/abvp-protest-in-du-s-ramjas-college-over-invite-to-jnu-students-umar-khalid-shehla-rashid/story-bV7V8uI1KmDoQNvID7A4VP.html (accessed June 2022).

Holmes, D. and G. Marcus. 2005. 'Cultures of Expertise and the Management of Globalization: Towards the Re-functioning of Ethnography'. In Aihwa Ong and Stephen J. Collier (eds), *Global Assemblages: Technology, Politics, and Ethics as Anthropological Problems*. Massachusetts: Blackwell.

Hoskin, Keith W. 1993. 'Education and the Genesis of Disciplinarity: The Unexpected Reversal'. In Ellen Messer-Davidow, David R. Shumway, and David J. Sylvan (eds), *Knowledges: Historical and Critical Studies in Disciplinarity*. Charlottesville: University Press of Virginia.

Human Rights Watch. 2014. '"They Say We're Dirty": Denying an Education to India's Marginalized'.

Hunter, Ian. 1996. 'Assembling the School'. In Andrew Barry, Thomas Osborne, and Nikolas Rose (eds), *Foucault and the Political Reason: Liberalism, neo-Liberalism, and Rationalities of Government*. London: University College.

Jain, Manish. 2018. 'Public, Private and Education: A Historical Overview'. In Manish Jain, Archana Mehendale, Rahul Mukhopadhyay, Padma M. Saranagapani and Christopher Winch (eds), *School Education In India: Market, State and Quality*. Oxon: Routledge.

Jeffrey, C. 2010. *Timepass: Youth, Class, and the Politics of Waiting in India*. Stanford: Stanford University Press.

Jeffrey, Craig, Roger Jeffery and Patricia Jeffery. 2004. 'Broken Trajectories: Dalit Young Men and Formal Education'. In Radhika Chopra and Patricia Jeffery (eds) in collaboration with Helmut Reifeld *Educational Regimes in Contemporary India*. Sage: New Delhi.

Jeffrey, Craig, Patricia Jeffery and Roger Jeffery. 2007. *Degrees without Freedom: Education, Masculinities, and Unemployment in North India*. California: Stanford University Press.

Jena, Shibsankar, 2007. 'The 'Village' in Postcolonial Development Discourse: India as a Case Study'. *Social Change and Development* 5(November).

Jha, Jyotsna and Dhir Jhingran. 2002. *Elementary Education for the Poorest and Other Disadvantaged Groups: The Real Challenge of Universalisation.* New Delhi: Centre for Policy Research.

John, Mary, Praveen Jha and Surinder Jodhka (eds). 2006. *Contested Transformations: Changing Economies and Identities in Contemporary India.* New Delhi: Tulika.

Jonathan, Ruth. 1989. 'Choices and Control in Education: Parental Rights, Individual Liberties and Social Justice'. *British Journal of Educational Studies,* Vol 37(4).

Joshi, Siddharth and Deepak Malghan. 2017. 'Faculty Diversity at the Indian Institutes of Management'. *Economic and Political Weekly* 52(13).

Kabeer, N., G. Nambissan, and R. Subrahmanian (eds). 2003. *Child Labour and the Right to Education in South Asia. Needs versus Rights?* New Delhi: Sage.

Kamat, Sangeetha, Carol Anne Spreen, and Indivar Jonnalagadda. 2016. *Profiting from the Poor: The Emergence of Multinational Edu-businesses in Hyderabad, India.* Amherst: University of Massachusetts.

Karabel, Jerome and A. H. Halsey. 1977. 'Introduction: Educational Research: A Review and Interpretation'. In Jerome Karabel and A. H. Halsey (eds), *Power and Ideology in Education.* New York: Oxford University Press.

Khilnani, Sunil. 1997. *The Idea of India.* London: Penguin.

Kingdon, Geeta Gandhi. 2007. 'The Progress of School Education in India', GPRG–WPS-071. Oxford: Global Poverty Research Group.

———. 1996. 'Private Schooling in India'. *Economic and Political Weekly* 31(6).

Kirpal, V and Meenakshi Gupta. 1999. *Equality through Reservations.* Jaipur: Rawat Publications.

Krishna, Anirudh. 2014. 'Examining the Structure of Opportunity and Social Mobility in India: Who Becomes an Engineer?' *Development and Change* 45(1).

Kumar, Krishna. 1985. 'Educational Experience of Scheduled Castes and Tribes'. In S. Shukla and Krishna Kumar (eds), *Sociological Perspectives in Education: A Reader.* Delhi: Chanakya Publications.

———. 1991. 'Meek Dictator: The Paradox of the Teacher's Personality'. In Krishna Kumar, *Political Agenda of Education: A Study of Colonist and Nationalist Ideas.* New Delhi: Sage.

———. 1992. *What is Worth Teaching?* Hyderabad: Orient Longman.

———. 1994. *Learning from Conflict*. New Delhi: Viking.

———. 1996. 'Two Worlds' In Krishna Kumar, *Learning from Conflict*. Hyderabad: Orient Longman.

———. 2001. *Prejudice and Pride: School Histories of the Freedom Struggle in India and Pakistan*. New Delhi: Viking.

———. 2003. 'Judicial Ambivalence and New Politics of Education'. *Economic and Political Weekly* 38(49).

Kumar, Nita. 2007. *The Politics of Gender, Community, and Modernity: Essays on Education in India*. New Delhi: Oxford University Press.

Kumar, Ravi. 2006. 'Introduction: Equality, Quality, and Quantity—Mapping the Challenges before Elementary Education in India'. In Ravi Kumar (ed.), *The Crisis of Elementary Education in India*. New Delhi: Sage.

Kumar, Satendar. 2014. 'Privatisation of Higher Education in India: Hopes and Despairs'. *Social Change* 44(3).

Kundu, Amitabh. 2006. 'Globalisation, Inequality and the Mobility of Populations in India'. In Mary John, Praveen Jha and Surinder Jodhka (eds), *Contested Transformations: Changing Economies and Identities in Contemporary India*. New Delhi: Tulika.

Lareau, A. 2003. *Unequal Childhoods: Class, Race, and Family Life*. Berkeley: University of California Press.

Li, Tani Murray. 1996. 'Images of Community: Discourse and Strategy in Property Relations'. *Development and Change* 27.

Livemint. 2020. 'Byju's onboards new investors, valuation now at $11.1 bn', 22 September. Available at https://www.livemint.com/companies/start-ups/byju-s-onboards-new-investors-valuation-now-at-11-1-bn-11600798077568.html (accessed May 2022).

Luke, Allan. 2000. 'New Narratives of Human Capital: Recent Redirections in Australian Educational Policy'. In Stephen J. Ball (ed.), *Sociology of Education: Major Themes, Vol I: Theories and Methods*. London: Routledge.

———. 2006. 'Teaching after the Market: From Commodity to Cosmopolitan'. In Lois Weis, Cameron McCarthy, and Greg Dimitriadis (eds), *Ideology, Curriculum, and the New Sociology of Education: Revisiting the Work of Michael Apple*. Routledge: London.

Maithreyi, R. 2018. 'Children's reconstruction of psychological knowledge: An ethnographic study of life skills programmes in India'. *Childhood* 26(1).

———. 2021. *Educating Youth: Regulation through Psychosocial Skilling in India*. New Delhi: Sage Publications Pvt. Ltd.

Majumdar, Manabi and Joos Mooij. 2011. *Education and Inequality, India: A Classroom View*, New Delhi: Routledge.

Malagatti, Aravind. 1994. *Government Brahmana*: *Ondu Atmacharitre* (Government Brahman: An Autobiography [in Kannada]). Kuvempu Institute of Kannada Studies, Manasagangotri: University of Mysore.

Mamdani, Mahmood. 2001. 'Beyond Settler and Native Political Identities: Overcoming the Political Legacy of Colonialism'. *Comparative Studies in Society and History* 43(4).

Manjrekar, Nandini. n. d. 'The Neighbourhood and the School: Conflict, Educational Marginalisation and the State in Contemporary Gujarat', TRG Poverty and Education Working Paper Series. New Delhi: Max Weber Stiftung.

Mathew, Leya. 2017. 'Betrayed futures: Uneconomic schooling in liberalizing Kerala (India)'. In A. Stambach and K. Hall (eds), *Anthropological perspectives of student futures: Youth and the politics of possibility*. London: Palgrave.

McGivney, Joseph and William Moynihan. 1972. 'School and Community'. *Teachers College Record* 74(2).

McLaren, Peter. 2009. 'Being, Becoming and Breaking-Free: Peter McLaren and the Pedagogy of Liberation' (Peter McLaren in an interview with Ravi Kumar). *Radical Notes,* 19 February.

Mezirow, Jack. 1978. 'Perspective transformation'. *Adult Education* 28(2): 100–110.

Mezirow, Jack et al. 2000. *Learning as Transformation.* San Francisco: Jossey-Bass.

Midgley, James. 1986. 'Introduction'. In James Midgley, Margaret Hardiman, and Dhanpaul Narine (eds), *Community Participation, Social Development and the State*. London: Methuen and co.

Moosvi, Ali Raza. 2012. 'The "discontents" must go', *The Hindu*, 8 October. Available at https://www.thehindu.com/features/education/issues/The-%E2%80%98discontents%E2%80%99-must-go/article12550042.ece (accessed April 2022).

Mukhopadhyay, Rahul. 2009. 'Changing Mindsets about Quality,' In Preet Rustagi (ed.), *Concerns, Conflicts, and Cohesions: Universalisation of Elementary Education in India*. New Delhi: Sage.

Mukhopadhyay, Rahul, S. Ramkumar, and A. R. Vasavi. 2007. 'Management Structures: Mid Project Review of EFA in India', Paper Submitted to the MHRD and NUEPA. New Delhi.

Mukhopadhyay, Rahul, N. Ramkumar and A. R. Vasavi. 2009. *Management of Elementary Education: Structures and Strategies.* New Delhi: NUEPA.

Muralidharan, Karthik and Venkatesh Sundararaman. 2013. 'The Aggregate Effect of School Choice. Evidence from a Two-Stage Experiment in India', Working Paper 19441. Washington: NBER.

Naik, J. P. 1975. *Equality, Quality and Quantity: The Elusive Triangle in Indian Education*. New Delhi: Allied Publishers.

Nair, Janaki. 2016. *The Provocations of the Public University in Contemporary India.* National Lecture in Memory of Shri. K. R. Narayanan. Kozhikode: CREST.

Nambissan, Geetha B. 2013. 'Opening Up the Black Box? Sociologists and the Study of Schooling in India'. In Geetha B. Nambissan and S. Srinivas Rao (eds), *Sociology of Education in India: Changing Contours and Emerging Concerns*. New Delhi: Oxford University Press.

———. 2014. 'Poverty, Markets and Elementary Education in India', TRG Poverty and Education Series Working Paper. New Delhi: Max Weber Stiftung.

Nambissan, Geetha B. and Mona Sedwal. 2002. 'Education for All: The Situation of Dalit Children in India'. In R. Govinda (ed.), *India Education Report: A Profile of Basic Education.* New Delhi: Oxford University Press.

Nampoothiri, D. D. 2011. 'Confronting Social Exclusion: A Critical Review of the CREST Experience', Manuscript. Kozhikode: CREST. Now published in Satish Deshpande and U. Zacharias (eds). 2013. *Beyond Inclusion: The Practice of Equal Access in Indian Higher Education*. London: Routledge

National Crime Records Bureau (NCRB). 2020. *Crime in India: 2020, Statistics: Vol I.* New Delhi: Ministry of Home Affairs. Available at https://ncrb.gov.in/sites/default/files/CII%202020%20Volume%201.pdf (accessed June 2022).

National Institute of Advanced Studies (NIAS). 2001a: 'Children's Double Burden: Livelihood and Schooling in a Fishing Community', Local Education Report: Chirala (Andhra Pradesh). National Institute of Advanced Studies: Bangalore.

———. 2001b. *Marginalised Communities and Dysfunctional Schools*, Local Education Report: Khategaon (Madhya Pradesh). National Institute of Advanced Studies: Bangalore.

———. 2001c. 'Discrimination and Deprivation: Basic Education among the Poor', Local Education Report: Jaipur (Rajasthan). Bangalore: National Institute of Advanced Studies: Bangalore.

———. 2002a. 'Urban Poverty and Schooling', Local Education Report for Bangalore. Bangalore: National Institute of Advanced Studies.

———. 2002b. 'Caste, Class, and Education Deprivation', Local Education Reports. Bangalore: National Institute of Advanced Studies.

———. 2007. 'School Community Contact Programme', Summary Report Submitted to Department of Education. Bangalore: National Institute of Advanced Studies.

National University of Educational Planning and Administration (NUEPA). 2011. *Elementary Education in India: Progress towards UEE*. DISE 2009–10. NUEPA: New Delhi.

———. 2014. *School Education in India: Flash Statistics*. DISE 2013–14. NUEPA: New Delhi.

Nayyar, Rohini and Alakh N. Sharma. 2005. *Rural Transformations in India: The Role of Non-Farm Sector*. Institute for Human Development: New Delhi.

NDTV. 2018. 'Bandh Called By Lawyers Supporting Accused In Jammu 8-Year-Old Rape, Murder', 12 April. Available at https://www.ndtv.com/india-news/kathua-rape-murder-bandh-called-by-lawyers-supporting-the-accused-in-the-case-1835770 (accessed April 2022).

Niranjanaradhya, V. P. n. d. 'Accountability and Transparency in School Education: School Development and Monitoring Committees in Karnataka', Manuscript. Bangalore: Centre for Child and Law. NLSIU.

———. 2019. 'The Draft Report to Evolve a National Education Policy Lacks Perspective to Build an Egalitarian Society Based on the Constitutional Values: A Constructive Critique', MS. Bengaluru: Centre for Child and Law; National Law School of India University.

Nisbet, Robert. 1967. *The Sociological Tradition*. London: Heinemann.

Noronha, Anjali. 2003. 'The Community in Charge: Shades of Experience From Madhya Pradesh'. In R. Govinda and Rashmi Diwan (eds), *Community Participation and Empowerment in Primary Education*. New Delhi: Sage.

Page, Elspeth. 2005. 'Negotiation and Compromise: Gender and Government Elementary Education'. In *Educational Regimes in Contemporary India*, Eds. Radhika Chopra and Patricia Jeffery in collaboration with HelmutReifeld. New Delhi: Sage.

Pathak, Avijit. 2021. 'Our children don't need a "deshbhakti" curriculum', *The Indian Express,* 28 October. Available at https://indianexpress.com/article/opinion/columns/children-dont-need-deshbhakti-curriculum-7592407/ (accessed June 2022).

Peters, Michael. A. 2009. 'Education, Creativity, and the Economics of Passions: New Forms of Educational Capitalism'. *Thesis Eleven* 96(Feb).

Piketty, Thomas. 2014. *Capital in the Twenty-First Century,* Arthur Goldhammer (trans.). Cambridge, Mass.: Belknap Press.

PROBE Team. 1999. *Public Report on Basic Education in India*. New Delhi: Oxford University Press.

Putnam, Robert. 1993. *Making Democracy Work: Civic Traditions in Modern Italy*. New Jersey: Princeton University Press.

Raina, Vinod. 2002. 'Decentralisation in Education' In *India Education Report: A Profile of Basic Education.* New Delhi: NIEPA.

Ramachandran, Vimala and Taramani Naorem. 2013. 'What It Means To Be a Dalit or Tribal Child in Our Schools'. *Economic and Political Weekly* 48(44).

Ramachandran, Vimala, Suman Bhattacharjea, and K. M. Sheshagiri. 2009. *Primary School Teachers: The Twists and Turns of Everyday Practice*. New Delhi: Education Resource Unit.

Rao, V. and M. Walton (eds). 2004. *Culture and Public Action*. Stanford: Stanford University Press.

Reimers, Fernando (ed.). 2000. *Unequal Schools, Unequal Chances: The Challenges to Equal Opportunity in the Americas*. Cambridge, MA: Harvard University Press.

Roy, Kumkum. 2019. 'Examining the Draft National Education Policy, 2019'. *Economic and Political Weekly, Engage* 54(25).

Sadgopal, Anil. 2011. 'Education Policy and RTE Bill: A Historical Betrayal'. In Harsh Dobhal (ed.), *Writings on Human Rights, Law and Society in India,* A Combat Law Anthology. Human Rights Legal Network. Available at http://www.samacheerkavi.in/pdf/CombatLaw_Anil_Sadgopal_Historical_Betrayal_Aug09.pdf (accessed June 2022).

Samaddar, Ranabir. 2019. 'Debate: What Are We Missing When Talking of Education in West Bengal?' *The Wire*, 09 July. Available at https://thewire.in/education/west-bengal-education-growth (accessed June 2022).

Sandel, Michel. J. 2020. *The Tyranny of Merit: What's Become of the Common Good?* New Delhi: Allen Lane/Penguin Books.

Sanyal, Kalyan. 2007. *Rethinking Capitalist Development: Primitive Accumulation, Governmentality, and Post-Colonial Capitalism.* New Delhi: Routledge.

Sarin, Ankur and Swati Gupta. 2013. 'Quotas under RTE: Leading towards an egalitarian education system?', IIMA Working Papers WP 2013-10-01. Indian Institute of Management Ahmedabad, Research and Publication Department.

Satish, Joseph. 2019. 'Jesuit Spirituality and Gandhian Praxis: Embracing an Interfaith Dialogue that Does Environmental Justice in India'. *Journal Of Rural Development* 38(3): 466–481. Available at DOI:10.25175/jrd/2019/v38/i3/147922 (accessed June 2022).

Schweder, Richard A. 2017. 'The End of the Modern Academy: At the University of Chicago, for Example'. *Social Research: An International Quarterly* 84(3).

Scroll.in. 2018. 'Ram Guha tweets that he isn't joining Ahmedabad University "due to circumstances beyond" his control', 01 November. Available at https://scroll.in/latest/900527/ram-guha-tweets-that-he-isnt-joining-ahmedabad-university-due-to-circumstances-beyond-his-control (accessed June 2022).

———. 2021. 'MP Police object to speakers, including DU professor Apoorvanand, invited for university webinar', 30 July. Available at https://scroll.in/latest/1001495/mp-police-object-to-speakers-invited-for-university-webinar-warn-against-law-and-order-problem (accessed May 2022).

Sharan, S. V. 2007. 'Primary Education and PRIs: Constitution and State Acts on Panchayats'. Paper presented at the conference on 'Role of PRI in Universalisation of Quality School Education' organised by the Aga Khan Foundation, and held at Jaipur, April.

Sharma, Rashmi. 2009. 'The Internal Dynamic'. In Rashmi Sharma and Vimala Ramachandran (eds), *Elementary Education System in India: Exploring Institutional Structures, Processes and Dynamics.* New Delhi: Routledge.

Shiva Kumar, A. K. and Preet Rustagi. 2010. *Elementary Education in India: Progress, Setbacks and Challenges.* New Delhi: Oxfam India.

Shukla, Sureshchandra. 1962. *The Context of Education in Developing Societies.* Delhi: Central Institute of Education.

Sikand, Yoginder. 2005. *Bastions of the Believers: Madrasas and Islamic Education in India.* New Delhi: Penguin.

Singh, K.S. 1992. *People of India,* Vol. I. New Delhi: Oxford University Press.

Sivaramakrishnan, K. 2000. 'Crafting the Public Sphere in the Forests of West Bengal: Democracy, Development and Political Action'. *American Ethnologist* 27(May).

Soudien, Crain. 2007. 'Caste, Class and Race: Continuities and Discontinuities across Indian and South African Schools'. *South African Historical Journal* 57.

———. *Realising the Dream: Unlearning the Logic of Race in the South African School.* Cape Town: HSRC Press.

Sriprakash, Arathi. 2011. 'Being a Teacher in Contexts of Change: Education Reform and the Re-positioning of Teachers' Work in India'. *Contemporary Education Dialogue* 8(1).

Star of Mysore. 2018. 'Finally, UGC Grants Recognition To 17 Courses Offered By KSOU', 10 August. Available at https://starofmysore.com/finally-ugc-grants-recognition-to-17-courses-offered-by-ksou/ (accessed June 2022).

Strain, Michael. 1995. 'Autonomy, Schools and the Constitutive Role of Community: Towards a New Moral and Political Order for Education'. *British Journal of Educational Studies* 43(1).

Subramanian, Ramya. 2000. 'Village Communities and the Achievement of Universal Primary Education: A Case Study from Karnataka'. In Naila Kabeer and Ramya Subramanian (eds), *Needs versus Rights? Child Labour and the Right to Education in South Asia.* New Delhi: Sage Publications.

Sundar, Nandini. 2017. *The Indian University Today: Our Intellectual and Professional Obligations.* Malcolm Adiseshaih Memorial Lecture. Chennai: Malcolm and Elizabeth Adiseshaiah Trust.

Swift-Morgan, J. 2006. 'What Community Participation in Schooling means: Insights from Southern Ethiopia'. *Harvard Educational Review* 76(3).

Tanabe, Akio. 2007. 'Toward Vernacular Democracy: Moral Social Society and Post-Postcolonial Transformation in Rural India'. *American Ethnologist* 34(3).

Tandon, Raj. 2002. *Primary Education and Panchayat Raj Institutions*. New Delhi: PRIA.

The Economic Times. 2015. 'University Grants Commission de-recognises KSOU for flouting norms', 18 June. Available at https://economictimes.indiatimes.com/industry/services/education/university-grants-commission-de-recognises-ksou-for-flouting-norms/articleshow/47726059.cms (accessed June 2022).

The Hindu. 2011. 'Ex-Information Commissioner H N Krishna remanded to judicial custody', 12 October. Available at https://www.thehindu.com/news/national/karnataka/exinformation-commissioner-h-n-krishna-remanded-to-judicial-custody/article2531947.ece (accessed June 2022).

———. 2012. 'New university to be named after Tipu Sultan', 04 November. Available at https://www.thehindu.com/features/education/college-and-university//article60016172.ece (accessed June 2022).

———. 2016. '20 per cent teacher aspirants clear Karnataka TET', 3 February. Available at https://www.thehindu.com/news/national/karnataka/20-per-cent-teacher-aspirants-clear-karnataka-tet/article8186847.ece (accessed June 2022).

———. 2019. 'Protest against 'Muslim' faculty continues in BHU', 19 November. Available at https://www.thehindu.com/news/national/protest-against-muslim-faculty-continues-in-bhu/article30019875.ece (accessed June 2022).

———. 2021a. 'Govt. drops prosecution of former chairman, ex-members of KPSC', 27 May. Available at https://www.thehindu.com/news/national/karnataka/govt-drops-prosecution-of-former-chairman-ex-members-of-kpsc/article34657125.ece (accessed June 2022).

———. 2021b. 'CBI files charge-sheet against 60 accused in Vyapam scam case', 8 January. Available at https://www.thehindu.com/news/national/cbi-files-charge-sheet-against-60-accused-in-vyapam-scam-case/article33523791.ece (accessed June 2022).

The New Indian Express. 2017. '793 kids dead in 10 years in Maharashtra's Ashram Schools; HC raps govt, bureaucrats', 12 June. Available at https://www.newindianexpress.com/cities/mumbai/2017/jun/12/793-kids-dead-in-10-years-in-maharashtras-ashram-schools-hc-raps-govt-bureaucrats-1615821.html (accessed June 2022).

The Wire. 2019. 'My Birth is My Fatal Accident: Rohith Vemula's Searing Letter is an Indictment of Social Prejudices', 17 January. Available at https://thewire.in/caste/rohith-vemula-letter-a-powerful-indictment-of-social-prejudices (accessed June 2022).

Therborn, G. 2009. 'The Killing-Fields of Inequality'. *Open Democracy,* 6 April. Available at https://www.opendemocracy.net/en/the-killing-fields-of-inequality/ (accessed June 2022).

Thorat, Sukhdeo and Khalid Khan. 2016. 'Private Sector and Equity in Higher Education Challenges of Growing Unequal Access'. In N. V. Varghese, Nidhi S. Sabharwal, and C. M. Malish (eds), *India Higher Education Report 2016: Equity.* SAGE Publishing.

Tilly, C. 1998. 'Changing Forms of Inequality'. *Sociological Theory* 21(1).

Tooley, J. and Pauline Dixon. 2005. *Private Education is Good for the Poor: A Study of Private Schools Serving the Poor in Low-Income Countries.* Washington, D.C.: Cato Institute.

Troyna, B. 2000. 'The Everyday World' of Teachers? Deracialised Discourses in the Sociology of Teachers and the Teaching Profession'. In Stephen J. Ball (ed.), *Sociology of Education: Major Themes, Vol. I: Theories and Methods.* London: Routledge.

Tyack, David E. 1977. 'City Schools: Centralisation of Control at the Turn of the Century'. In Jerome Karabel and A. H. Halsey (eds), *Power and Ideology in Education.* New York: Oxford University Press.

UGC (University Grants Commission). 2012. Statistics at a Glance. New Delhi: Ministry of Human Resource Development.

———. 2022. 'Total no. of universities in the country as on 24. 06. 2022'. Available at https://www.ugc.ac.in/oldpdf/Consolidated%20list%20of%20All%20Universities.pdf?_gl=1*zwvz1e*_ga*MTQ2NTEwODYyNC4xNjUyNTQ4MzQx*_ga_FGHYECNLXB*MTY1NTEwOTE2MC4yLjAuMTY1NTEwOTE2MC4w (accessed June 2022).

UNESCO. 1997. *Challenges of 'Education for All' in Asia and the Pacific and the APPEAL Response.* Bangkok: UNESCO Regional office.

———. 2021. *Reimagining our Futures Together: A New Social Contract for Education.* UNESCO: Paris.

Upadhya, Carol. 2001. 'The Concept of Community in Indian Social Sciences: An Anthropological Perspective'. In Mary John, Praveen Jha, and Surinder Jodhka (eds), *Community and Identities: Contemporary Discourses on Culture and Politics in India.* New Delhi: Tulika.

———. 2004. 'Capital Flows, Business Networks and Entrepreneurs in the Indian Software Industry', *Economic and Political Weekly* 39(48).

———. 2007. 'Employment, exclusion and 'merit' in the Indian IT industry'. *Economic and Political Weekly* 42(20).

Vaidyanathan, A. and P. R. Gopinathan Nair (eds). 2001. *Elementary Education in Rural India: Strategies for Human Development in India,* Vol. 2. New Delhi: Sage.

Van Gorder, Chris. 2008. 'Paulo Freire's Pedagogy for the Children of the Oppressors: Educating for Social Justice among the World's Privileged.' *Journal of Pedagogy, Pluralism, and Practice* 4(1). Available at https://digitalcommons.lesley.edu/jppp/vol4/iss1/6/ (accessed April 2022).

Vasavi, A. R. 2003. 'Schooling for a New Society: The Social and Political Bases of Education Deprivation in India'. In Ramya Subramanian, Yusuf Sayed, Sarada Balagopalan and Crain Soudien (eds), *Education Inclusion and Exclusion: Indian and South African Perspectives*, IDS Bulletin 34(1).

———. 2006a. 'Caste Indignities and Subjected Personhoods'. *Economic and Political Weekly* 41(35).

———. 2006b. 'An Emergent New Rurality: Some Reflections from Schools'. In Mary John et al. (eds), *Contested Transformations: Changing Economies and Identities in Contemporary India*, New Delhi: Tulika.

———. 2011. 'Pluralising the Sociology of India', *Contributions to Indian Sociology* 45(3): 399–426.

———. 2012. *Shadow Space: Suicides and the Predicament of Rural India.* Gurgaon: Three Essays Collective.

———. 2017. 'Government Brahmin: Caste, the Educated Unemployed and the Reproduction of Caste Inequalities', Transnational Research Group (TRG): Poverty and Education in India, Working Paper Series. London: German Historical Institute. Available at https://www.ghil.ac.uk/fileadmin/redaktion/dokumente/trg_india/Paper_1_A_R_Vasavi.pdf (accessed June 2022).

Vasavi, A. R. 2018. 'The Displaced Threshing Yard: Involutions of the Rural'. Malcolm Adiseshiah Memorial Lecture. Chennai: Malcolm and Elizabeth Adisehiah Trust.

———. 2019a. 'School Differentiation in India Reinforces Social Inequalities'. *The India Forum* April 12.

———. 2019b. 'The Displaced Threshing Yard: Involutions of the Rural'. *Review of Development and Change* 24(1): 31–54.

———. 2020. 'Re-thinking Mass Higher Education: Towards Community Integrated Learning'. Background Paper for the 'Futures of Education Initiative'. Paris: UNESCO.

Veerabhadranaika, P., Revathi Sampath Kumaran, Shivali Tukdeo and A. R. Vasavi. 2012. *The 'Education Question' from the Perspectives of Adivasis: Condition, Policies, and Structures*. Bangalore: National Institute of Advanced Studies and UNICEF.

Velaskar, Padma. 2013. 'Sociology of Educational Inequality in India: A Critique and a New Research Agenda'. In Geeta B. Nambissan and S. Srinivas Rao (eds), *Sociology of Education in India: Changing Contours and Emerging Concerns*. New Delhi: Oxford University Press.

Vicziany, Marika. 2005. 'Dalit Response to Unemployment in Contemporary India', *South Asia: Journal of South Asian Studies* XXVIII(1).

Weis, Lois and Michelle Fine. 2012. 'Critical Bifocality and Circuits of Privilege: Expanding Critical Ethnographic Theory and Design'. *Harvard Educational Review* 82(2).

Weis, Lois, Cameron McCarthy, and Greg Dimitriadis (eds). 2006. *Ideology, Curriculum and the New Sociology of Education*. London: Routledge.

Weisskopf, Thomas. 2004. *Affirmative Action in the United States and India: A Comparative Perspective*. New York: Routledge.

Whitty, Geoff. 1998. 'Citizens or Consumers? Continuity and Change in Contemporary Education Policy'. In D. Carlson and M. Apple (eds), *Critical Educational Theory in Unsettling Times*. Boulder, Co: Westview Press.

Wilson, Fiona. 2001. 'In the Name of the State? Schools and Teachers in an Andean Province'. In Thomas Blom Hansen and Finn Stepputatt (eds), *States of Imagination: Ethnographic Explorations of the Postcolonial State*. Durham: Duke University Press.

World Bank. 2006. *World Development Report, 2006.* Washington D.C.: World Bank.

Young, Jock. 2007. 'Holding Chaos in Abeyance: The Maintenance of Order amongt Lightly Engaged Strangers'. In Jock Young, *The Exclusive Society: Social Exclusion, Crime and Difference in Late Modernity*. SAGE publications.

INDEX